THE
PARABLES OF THE KINGDOM

Charles Harold Dodd was born in 1884. He went
up to Oxford with a classical scholarship.
Graduating in 1901 he became a research
scholar of Magdalen College. Turning from
ancient history to theology, he studied for the
ministry at Mansfield College, Oxford, and was
ordained in 1912. In 1930 he was appointed to
the Rylands Chair of Biblical Criticism and
Exegesis at Manchester University. Retiring in
1949 he became Chairman of the Translating
Committee for the new translation of the Bible.
He was a Fellow of the British Academy and an
honorary Fellow of University College, Oxford
and of Jesus College, Cambridge. He died in
1973.

His other books in this series are
THE EPISTLE OF PAUL TO THE ROMANS
THE MEANING OF PAUL FOR TODAY
THE AUTHORITY OF THE BIBLE

C. H. DODD

_____

The Parables
of the
Kingdom

Collins
FOUNT PAPERBACKS

First published by James Nisbet and Company 1935
Revised edition published by James Nisbet 1961
Revised edition first issued in Fontana Books 1961
Reprinted in Fount Paperbacks 1978
Fourth Impression October 1983

© C. H. Dodd 1961
© Preface C. F. D. Moule 1978

Made and printed in Great Britain by
William Collins Sons & Co Ltd Glasgow

REVERENDO ORDINI THEOLOGORVM

VNIVERSITATIS YALENSIS

APVD PORTVM NOVVM IN NOVA ANGLIA

HOSPITIBVS HOSPES

CONLEGIS CONLEGA

PREFACE

It was the greatness of this influential little book that, making extended use of " form-critical " methods for examining the pre-literary stages of Christian tradition, it offered a detailed interpretation of the teaching of Jesus as vitally related to the actual circumstances of his ministry and drew from it a coherent account of his understanding of history. The great German scholar William Wrede[1] had proposed theories that would virtually have demolished the gospel according to Mark as history; while Albert Schweitzer's interpretation[2] of the Gospel traditions had presented Jesus himself as heroically pinning his faith to an imminent apocalypse which failed to materialize. In the book which is now reprinted, C. H. Dodd looked for an alternative interpretation of the New Testament evidence, and found it through critical re-examination of the Gospel traditions which led him to see in Jesus and his ministry the key to history.

As Dodd read the evidence, Jesus was declaring that, in his ministry and teaching, in his very presence and in the crisis that it brought, God's reign, the Kingdom of God, had actually come: " Something has happened, which has not happened before, and which means that the sovereign power of God has come into effective operation " (p. 36). In other words, the sovereignty of God was not waiting to be more effectively in operation in the future: nothing within subsequent history was going to bring in the Kingdom more completely than had

[1] *Das Messiasgeheimnis in den Evangelien. Zugleich ein Beitrag zum Verständnis des Markusevangeliums* (Göttingen 1901, ³1963); Eng. trans. by J. C. G. Greig, *The Messianic Secret* (London: Clarke 1971)

[2] *Von Reimarus zu Wrede. Eine Geschichte der Leben-Jesu-Forschung* (Tübingen 1906); Eng. trans. by W. Montgomery, *The Quest of the Historical Jesus: A Critical Study of its Progress from Reimarus to Wrede* (London: A. and C. Black, ¹1910, ⁸1954).

already been the case in the coming of Jesus. With Jesus the *eschaton*, the final event, had come.

There is, it is true, a future tense in certain parts of the message of Jesus. One only needs to think of "thy Kingdom come" in the Lord's Prayer. But such future tenses, Dodd believed, related either to the subsequent consequences in history of what was already happening (for instance, the fall of Jerusalem and the persecution of Jesus' followers), or else to a transcendental consummation of God's purposes beyond history. If this was the case, then it was not Jesus but the Church that subsequently confused the issue by introducing into sayings attributed to Jesus (for instance, in the apocalyptic discourses)[3] references to a-temporal realities as though they were events of future history, and that began to speak of a *second* coming of Christ. Jesus' own message was of only one coming within history, and that, in his own ministry. So far as it can be realized in history, this already was the coming of the Kingdom, this already was the ultimate. Whatever in the genuine teaching of Jesus is still in the future tense was either a reference to the historical consequence of this coming, or else a pictorial way of referring to a consummation beyond history. In this respect, Dodd was inclined to believe that the Fourth Gospel had preserved, better than the Synoptic tradition, the original emphasis of Jesus himself.

He allowed that "realized eschatology" was not a very felicitous phrase,[4] and subsequently accepted as preferable Georges Florovsky's "inaugurated eschatology" or Joachim Jeremias' *sich realisierende Eschatologie*.[5] But he never altered his essential position. The revised edition (1961) of his book here

[3] Page 115

[4] Page 8

[5] See *The Interpretation of the Fourth Gospel* (Cambridge: University Press 1953), 447n. 1: "Emendations of it" [the phrase "realized eschatology"] "which have been suggested for the avoidance of misunderstandings are Professor Georges Florovsky's 'inaugurated eschatology' and Professor Joachim Jeremias' *sich realisierende Eschatologie*, which I like but cannot translate into English."

reprinted only made small alterations and added references. A
paper published in 1947[6] suggested that in both Paul and the
Gospel according to Matthew it was possible to find some
recognition of a Kingdom of Christ as a kind of first instal-
ment of the Kingdom of God, so that, in certain respects, the
Kingdom of God was yet to come; but this was not a substantial modification, nor irreconcilable with his original
thesis.

In this book Dodd was largely pioneering. It is true that he
was following Adolf Jülicher[7] in rejecting the allegorical
interpretation of parables. Much nearer home, A. T. Cadoux[8]
had anticipated him in relating the message of the parables to
the circumstances of Jesus himself. But nobody until then had
made a sustained exegetical study of the parables and sayings
of Jesus so as to deduce from it clear conclusions about
eschatology. He was followed by Joachim Jeremias[9], Eta
Linnemann[10], and others with technically more elaborate re-
constructions, and by J. A. T. Robinson[11] with a fuller account
of how the early Church's eschatology developed from the
teaching of Jesus. But Dodd's book is constantly referred back
to as a landmark in the investigation. As A. M. Hunter has
said[12], he " made exegetical history ", and " it is unthinkable
that there should be any retreat from Dodd's basic insights ";
and Jeremias has generously echoed this view (op. cit p.9).

Dodd has been criticized for his consistently " realized"
interpretation of the eschatology of Jesus and for applying the

[6] " Matthew and Paul ", a paper communicated to the Cambridge
Theological Society, 20th February, 1947, Expository Times lviii (1946-7),
293ff
[7] Die Gleichnisreden Jesu (Freiburg/Leipzig/Tübingen: Mohr 1899)
[8] The Parables of Jesus: their Art and Use (London: Clarke n.d.)
[9] Die Gleichnisse Jesu (Göttingen: Vandenhoeck und Ruprecht [6]1962);
Eng. trans. by S. H. Hooke, The Parables of Jesus (London: S.C.M. [2]1963)
[10] Gleichnisse Jesu: Einführung und Auslegung (Göttingen: Vandenhoeck
und Ruprecht 1961); Eng. trans. by J. Sturdy, Parables of Jesus: Introduction and Exposition (London: S.P.C.K. 1966)
[11] Jesus and His Coming (London: S.C.M. 1957)
[12] Interpreting the Parables (London: S.C.M. 1960), 39

parables exclusively to the crisis of Jesus' own day. Werner Kümmel[13] took issue with him for eliminating future references or interpreting them as referring to what was outside history, holding that, whatever the difficulties for the modern reader, Jesus himself in fact looked for a future coming of the Kingdom within history. Certainly I would agree, for my part, with those who do not find it natural to interpret the parables of growth to mean that the harvest has already arrived, and who believe that it is open to question whether some of the parables, even as Jesus himself told them, did not concern a future crises rather than the present. Dodd's interpretation of ἤγγικεν to mean "is already here" has been widely challenged, and so has his attempt to make "shall see the Kingdom come" mean " shall see that the Kingdom had come " (Mark 9:1). A good deal of more recent work on the parables is striking out in quite different directions, and investigating parable as a literary form, or treating it as a " speech-event " independent of its original context.[14] But, so far as attempts to recover the Jesus of history are concerned, Dodd has rendered a permanent service in showing him as no generalizing moralist (like Adolf Jülicher's Jesus), but as addressing himself, there and then, and with the most stringent urgency, to the crisis which his own person and ministry constituted.

The lectures on which the book was based were delivered at Yale in the spring of 1935. In the autumn of the same prolific year another course of lectures was delivered which became The Apostolic Preaching and its Developments (London: Hodder and Stoughton 1936), telling how Jesus was interpreted in the early apostolic message. A single paper, delivered

[13] Verheissung und Erfüllung (Zürich: Zwingli [3]1956); Eng. trans. by D. M. Barton, Promise and Fulfilment (London: S.C.M. 1957)

[14] E.g. E. Fuchs, E. Jüngel, R. W. Funk. See C. W. F. Smith, The Jesus of the Parables (Philadelphia: United Church Press [2]1975); and, for the earlier story, G. V. Jones, The Art and Truth of the Parables (London: S.P.C.K. 1964). A short monograph to which I am also indebted is E. E. Wolfzorn, Realized Eschatology: an Exposition of Charles H. Dodd's Thesis (Publications Universitaires de Louvain/Desclée de Brouwer 1962). (C. H. Dodd was actually called " Harold ", not " Charles ".)

on 24th October 1935, and incorporated in that book, sum-
marized the philosophy of history implied in both books; and
this was unfolded in more detail in *History and the Gospel*
(London: Nisbet 1938). But among these the book on the
parables is outstanding. Written in Dodd's characteristically
terse, lucid, jargon-free style, with masterly simplicity, it is so
persuasive that one has to struggle hard to be objectively
critical; and, even if at length one manages to resist the spell
enough to disagree, it remains illuminating and instructive;
and, for all its sweet reasonableness and restraint, it is an
almost passionate confession of a great scholar's lifelong conviction. It is good that it should be reprinted.

C. F. D. MOULE
Cambridge February 1976

CONTENTS

Chapter I

THE NATURE AND PURPOSE OF
THE GOSPEL PARABLES

The parables are perhaps the most characteristic element in
the teaching of Jesus Christ as recorded in the Gospels. They
have upon them, taken as a whole, the stamp of a highly
individual mind, in spite of the re-handling they have inevitably suffered in the course of transmission. Their appeal to
the imagination fixed them in the memory, and gave them
a secure place in the tradition. Certainly there is no part of
the Gospel record which has for the reader a clearer ring of
authenticity.

But the interpretation of the parables is another matter.
Here there is no general agreement. In the traditional teaching
of the Church for centuries they were treated as allegories, in
which each term stood as a cryptogram for an idea, so that
the whole had to be de-coded term by term. A famous example
is Augustine's interpretation of the parable of the Good Samaritan.

A certain man went down from Jerusalem to Jericho; Adam
himself is meant; *Jerusalem* is the heavenly city of peace,
from whose blessedness Adam fell; *Jericho* means the moon,
and signifies our mortality, because it is born, waxes, wanes,
and dies. *Thieves* are the devil and his angels. *Who stripped
him,* namely, of his immortality; *and beat him,* by persuading
him to sin; *and left him half-dead,* because in so far as man
can understand and know God, he lives, but in so far as he
is wasted and oppressed by sin, he is dead; he is therefore
called *half-dead.* The *priest and Levite* who saw him and
passed by, signify the priesthood and ministry of the *Old
Testament,* which could profit nothing for salvation. *Samaritan* means Guardian, and therefore the Lord Himself is signi-
fied by this name. The *binding* of the wounds is the restraint
of sin. *Oil* is the comfort of good hope; *wine* the exhortation
to work with fervent spirit. The *beast* is the flesh in which

He designed to come to us. The being *set upon the beast* is belief in the incarnation of Christ. The *inn* is the Church, where travellers returning to their heavenly country are refreshed after pilgrimage. The *morrow* is after the resurrection of the Lord. The *two pence* are either the two precepts of love, or the promise of this life and of that which is to come. The *innkeeper* is the Apostle (Paul). The supererogatory payment is either his counsel of celibacy, or the fact that he worked with his own hands lest he should be a burden to any of the weaker brethren when the Gospel was new, though it was lawful for him " to live by the Gospel."—(*Quaestiones Evangeliorum,* II, 19—slightly abridged.)

This interpretation of the parable in question prevailed down to the time of Archbishop Trench, who follows its main lines with even more ingenious elaboration; and it is still to be heard in sermons. To the ordinary person of intelligence who approaches the Gospels with some sense for literature this mystification must appear quite perverse.

Yet it must be confessed that the Gospels themselves give encouragement to this allegorical method of interpretation. Mark interprets the parable of the Sower, and Matthew those of the Tares and the Dragnet, on just such principles; and both attribute their interpretations to Jesus Himself. It was the great merit of Adolph Jülicher, in his work *Die Gleichnisreden Jesu* (1899-1910) that he applied a thoroughgoing criticism to this method, and showed, not that the allegorical interpretation is in this or that case overdone or fanciful, but that the parables in general do not admit of this method at all, and that the attempts of the evangelists themselves to apply it rest on a misunderstanding.

The crucial passage is Mk. iv. 11-20. Jesus, in answer to a question of His disciples, says : " To you is granted the mystery of the Kingdom of God, but to those outside everything comes in parables, in order that they may look and look but never see, listen and listen but never understand, lest they should be converted and forgiven "; and then follows the interpretation of the parable of the Sower. Now this whole passage is strikingly unlike in language and style to the majority of the sayings of Jesus. Its vocabulary includes (within this short space) seven words which are not proper to the rest of the Synoptic record.[1] All seven are characteristic of the vocabulary of Paul, and most of them occur also in other apostolic writers. These facts create at once a presumption that we have here not a part of the primitive tradition of the words of Jesus, but a piece of apostolic teaching.

Further, the interpretation offered is confused. The seed is the Word: yet the crop which comes up is composed of various classes of people. The former interpretation suggests the Greek idea of the "seminal word"; while the latter is closely akin to a similitude in the Apocalypse of Ezra: "As the farmer sows over the ground many seeds, and plants a multitude of plants, but in the season not all that have been planted take root, so also of those who have sowed in the world not all shall be saved" (II Esdras viii. 41). Two inconsistent lines of interpretation have been mixed up. Yet we may suppose that the Teller of the parable knew exactly what He meant by it.

Again, the idea that the parable is a veiled revelation of the coming behaviour of those who heard the teaching of Jesus, under temptation and persecution, is bound up with the view expressed in 11-12 about the purpose of parables. According to these verses they were spoken in order to prevent those who were not predestined to salvation from understanding the teaching of Jesus. This is surely connected with the doctrine of the primitive Church, accepted with modifications by Paul, that the Jewish people to whom Jesus came were by divine providence blinded to the significance of His Coming, in order that the mysterious purpose of God might be fulfilled through their rejection of the Messiah. That is to say, this explanation of the purpose of the parables is an answer to a question which arose after the death of Jesus, and the failure of His followers to win the Jewish people. But that He desired not to be understood by the people in general, and therefore clothed His teaching in unintelligible forms, cannot be made credible on any reasonable reading of the Gospels.

[1] Μυστήριον, οἱ ἔξω, πρόσκαιρος, ἀπάτη are not found in the Synoptics outside this passage; ἐπιθυμία is found elsewhere only in Lk. xxii. 15, in a different sense; διωγμός and θλῖψις are found only in Mk. x. 30, and in the Synoptic Apocalypse (Mk. xiii.), passages which are for other reasons suspected of being secondary.

The probability is that the parables could have been taken for allegorical mystifications only in a non-Jewish environment. Among Jewish teachers the parable was a common and well-understood method of illustration, and the parables of Jesus are similar in form to Rabbinic parables. The question therefore, why He taught in parables, would not be likely to arise, still less to receive such a perplexing answer. In the Hellenistic world, on the other hand, the use of myths, allegorically interpreted, as vehicles of esoteric doctrine, was widespread, and something of the kind would be looked for from Christian teachers. It was this, as much as anything, which set interpretation going on wrong lines.

What then are the parables, if they are not allegories? They are the natural expression of a mind that sees truth in concrete pictures rather than conceives it in abstractions. The contrast between the two ways of thinking may be illustrated from two passages in the Gospels. In Mk. xii. 33 a scribe is introduced, who expresses the sentiment: "To love one's neighbour as oneself is better than all burnt offerings and sacrifices." In Mt. v. 23 the same idea is expressed thus: "If you are offering your gift at the altar, and remember there and then that your brother has something against you, leave your gift there before the altar, and go and get reconciled with your brother first of all; then come and offer your gift." This concrete, pictorial mode of expression is thoroughly characteristic of the sayings of Jesus. Thus instead of saying, "Beneficence should not be ostentatious," He says, "When you give alms, do not blow your trumpet"; instead of saying, "Wealth is a grave hindrance to true religion," He says, "It is easier for a camel to go through the eye of a needle than for a rich man to enter the Kingdom of God." In such figurative expression the germ of the parable is already present.

At its simplest the parable is a metaphor or simile drawn from nature or common life, arresting the hearer by its vividness or strangeness, and leaving the mind in sufficient doubt about its precise application to tease it into active thought. Our common language is full of dead metaphors: a thought "strikes" us; young men "sow wild oats"; politicians "explore avenues." Such dead metaphors are often a sign of mental laziness and a substitute for exact thought. But a living metaphor is another thing. " Where the carcass is the vultures will gather "; " a town set on a mountain cannot be hidden "; " make yourselves purses that do not wear out "; " if the blind lead the blind, both fall into the ditch."

Now such a simple metaphor may be elaborated into a picture, by the addition of detail. Thus : " They do not light a lamp and put it under the meal-tub, but on a lamp-stand; and then it gives light to all in the house "; " No one sews a patch of unshrunk cloth on an old coat, else the patch pulls away from it—the new from the old—and there is a worse tear "; " Why do you look at the splinter in your brother's eye, without noticing the plank in your own eye? How can you say to your brother, let me take the splinter out of your eye, when there is a plank in your own?"; or take a simile, " To what shall I compare this generation? It is like children sitting in the market-place and calling to one another, we played the pipes for you and you would not dance; we set up a wail for you and you would not weep ! " This is the type of parable which is called by the Germans *Gleichnis,* i.e. similitude. It is a common type, including, for example, the Son asking for Bread, the Eye the Light of the Body, the Sons of the Bridechamber, the Fig-tree as Herald of Summer (Mk. xiii. 29), and other familiar parables.

Or again, the metaphor (or simile) may be elaborated into a story instead of a picture, the additional details serving to develop a situation. This is what the Germans call *Parabel,* the parable proper. The story may be a very short one; e.g. " The Kingdom of God is like leaven which a woman took and hid in three measures of meal, until the whole was leavened." Very little longer are the parables of the Lost Sheep and Lost Coin, the Hid Treasure and the Costly Pearl, the Mustard-Seed, the Seed Growing Secretly and the Two Sons. Somewhat longer are the Two Houses, the Sower, the Importunate Friend, and some others. And finally we have full-length tales (" Novellen ") like the Money in Trust, the Unforgiving Servant (Mt. xviii. 23-35), the Prodigal Son, and the Labourers in the Vineyard.

It cannot be pretended that the line can be drawn with

any precision between these three classes of parable—figurative sayings, similitudes, and parables proper.[2] If we say that the first class has no more than one verb, the second more than one verb, in the present tense, and the third a series of verbs in an historic tense, we have a rough grammatical test; and this corresponds to the fact that the similitude on the whole tends to describe a typical or recurrent case, the parable a particular case treated as typical. But one class melts into another, and it is clear that in all of them we have nothing but the elaboration of a single comparison, all the details being designed to set the situation or series of events in the clearest possible light, so as to catch the imagination.

This leads us at once to the most important principle of interpretation. The typical parable, whether it be a simple metaphor, or a more elaborate similitude, or a full-length story, presents one single point of comparison. The details are not intended to have independent significance. In all allegory, on the other hand, each detail is a separate metaphor, with a significance of its own. Thus in the *Pilgrim's Progress* we have the episode of the House Beautiful. It is a story of the arrival of belated travellers at a hospitable country house. Commentators even undertake to show us the actual house in Bedfordshire. But in the story the maid who opens the door is Discretion, the ladies of the house are Prudence, Piety and Charity, and the bedchamber is Peace. Or to take a biblical example, in Paul's allegory of the Christian warrior the girdle is Truth, the breastplate Righteousness, the shoes Peace, the shield Faith, the helmet Salvation, and the sword the Word of God. On the other hand, if we read the parable of the Importunate Friend, it would be obviously absurd to ask who is represented by the friend who arrives from a journey, or the children who are in bed. These and all the other details of the story are there simply to build up the picture of a sudden crisis of need, calling for an urgency which would otherwise be untimely and even impertinent.

[2] This is Bultmann's basis of classification; Bildwörter, Gleichnisse, and Parabel, see *Geschichte der synoptischen Tradition*, 1931, pp. 179-222.

Similarly in the parable of the Sower the wayside and the birds, the thorns and the stony ground are not, as Mark supposed, cryptograms for persecution, the deceitfulness of riches, and so forth. They are there to conjure up a picture of the vast amount of wasted labour which the farmer must face, and so to bring into relief the satisfaction that the harvest gives, in spite of all.

The object before the writer of an allegory is of course to tell his tale so that it reads naturally as such, even when the interpretation is out of sight. But this needs great skill, and it is scarcely possible to keep it up for long. The interpretation will show through. Thus to return to the House Beautiful, Bunyan has shown great skill in introducing the natural incidents of a short stay at a country house. Among other things, the ladies display, very naturally, the family pedigree, which one still sees framed and hung in some old-fashioned houses. But here theology breaks in : the pedigree showed that the Lord of the house "was the Son of the Ancient of Days, and came by an eternal generation." With less skilful allegorists the story often becomes sheer nonsense, and to make sense of it the details must be transposed into the idea which they signify. Thus Paul, who is not always felicitous in his use of illustration, gives an allegorical story of a gardener who lopped off the branches of an olive tree, and grafted in their place shoots of wild olive. The lopped branches, however, he kept by him, and after the wild grafts had " taken " he once more grafted the olive-branches into the stock (Rom. xi. 16-24). A curious piece of horticulture ! But it is all intelligible if we bear in mind that the olive-tree is the people of God; the lopped branches, the unbelieving Jews; the wild-olive shoots, the Gentile Christians.

In the parables of the Gospels, however, all is true to nature and to life. Each similitude or story is a perfect picture of something that can be observed in the world of our experience. The processes of nature are accurately observed and recorded; the actions of persons in the stories are in character; they are either such as anyone would recognize as natural in the circumstances, or, if they are surprising, the point of the parable is that such actions *are* surprising. Thus there is no doubt something surprising in the conduct of the employer who pays the same wages for one hour's work as for twelve, but the surprise of the labourers at being treated so gives point to the story.

In making this distinction between the parable and the allegory, we must not be too rigorous. For if the parable is drawn out to any length, it is likely that details will be inserted which are suggested by their special appropriateness to the application intended, and if the application is correctly made by the hearer, he will then see a secondary significance in these details. But in the true parable any such details will be kept strictly subordinate to the dramatic realism of the story, and will not disturb its unity. And this is, with very few exceptions, true of the parables given in the Gospels. Here and there interpretation has intruded itself into a parable and marred its realism. But if the parables are taken as a whole, their realism is remarkable. I have shown elsewhere[3] what a singularly complete and convincing picture the parables give of life in a small provincial town—probably a more complete picture of *petit-bourgeois* and peasant life than we possess for any other province of the Roman Empire except Egypt, where papyri come to our aid.

There is a reason for this realism of the parables of Jesus. it arises from a conviction that there is no mere analogy, but an inward affinity, between the natural order and the spiritual order; or as we might put it in the language of the parables themselves, the Kingdom of God is intrinsically *like* the process of nature and of the daily life of men. Jesus therefore did not feel the need of making up artificial illustrations for the truths He wished to teach. He found them ready-made by the Maker of man and nature. That human life, including the religious life, is a part of nature is distinctly stated in the well-known, passage beginning " Consider the fowls of the air. . . ." (Mt. vi. 26-30; Lk. xii. 24-28). Since nature and super-nature are one order, you can take any part of that order and find in it illumination for other parts. Thus the falling of rain is a religious thing, for it is God who makes the rain to fall on the just and the unjust; the death of a sparrow can be contemplated without despairing of the goodness of nature, because the bird is " not forgotten by your

[3] *The Authority of the Bible*, pp. 148-152.

Father "; and the love of God is present in the natural affection of a father for his scapegrace son. This sense of the divineness of the natural order is the major premiss of all the parables, and it is the point where Jesus differs most profoundly from the outlook of the Jewish apocalyptists, with whose ideas He had on some sides much sympathy. The orthodox Rabbis of the Talmud are also largely free from the gloomy pessimism of apocalypse, and hence they can produce true parables where the apocalyptists can give us only frigid allegories; but their minds are more scholastic, and their parables often have a larger element of artificiality than those of the Gospels.

A further point of contrast between the parable and the allegory is that while the allegory is a merely decorative illustration of teaching supposed to be accepted on other grounds, the parable has the character of an argument, in that it entices the hearer to a judgment upon the situation depicted, and then challenges him, directly or by implication, to apply that judgment to the matter in hand.[4] We need only recall a familiar and typical parable in the Old Testament, where Nathan tells David the story of the poor man's ewe lamb which was stolen by the rich man. David falls neatly into the trap, exclaiming indignantly, " As the Lord liveth, the man that hath done this is worthy to die"; whereupon Nathan retorts: " Thou art the man!" That the parables of Jesus had a similar intention is sometimes shown by the way in which they are introduced. Thus: "What do you think? if a man has a hundred sheep. . . ." "What do you think? A man had two children; he came to the first and said: My boy, go and work in the vineyard to-day. He answered, Yes, sir; but did not go. He went to the second and said the same. He answered, I will not; but afterwards he changed his mind and went. Which of the two did his father's will?" But whether they are so introduced or not, the question is implicit. The way to an interpretation lies through a judgment on the imagined situation, and not through the decoding of the various elements in the story.

[4] This argumentative character of the parable is emphasized by Bultmann (*Geschichte der synoptischen Tradition*, 1931, p. 195). It is well worked out by A. T. Cadoux, *The Parables of Jesus*, a very interesting book to which I am indebted, and to which I shall have other occasions to refer, though I cannot always accept his interpretations.

Jülicher and his followers, then, have done great service in teaching us how to take the first step towards the understanding of the parables. It is to accept the story as a piece of real life, and form our judgment upon it. What is the next step? Those who follow Jülicher's method tend to make the process of interpretation end with a generalization. Thus we may take the parable of the Money in Trust (Talents or Pounds). It is a story of a man whom overcaution or cowardice led into breach of trust. Such conduct is contemptible and befits no honourable man. That is our judgment on the situation. What then is the application? "We must vote for the broadest possible application," says Jülicher[5]; "fidelity in all that God has entrusted to us." By taking this line, he has happily delivered us from questions whether the talents represent the Gospel, the true doctrine, ecclesiastical offices, or bodily and spiritual capacities, with which the earlier exegetes concerned themselves; and equally from modern attempts to make the parable into an instruction to Christians to invest their money wisely, and incidentally into a justification for the capitalist system! But can we really be content with the pure generalization which Jülicher produces as the moral of the parable? Is it much more than an ethical commonplace?

Similarly the parable of the Sower leads to the judgment that in agriculture, much labour may be lost and yet a good harvest may be reaped. Are we to apply this in the form of the generalization that any kind of religious work is subject to the same conditions? Or shall we say that the parable of the Hid Treasure teaches that one should always sacrifice a lower good for a higher; that of the Waiting Servants that one should be prepared for emergencies; and that of the Lamp and the Bushel that truth will out? This method of interpretation makes the parables to be forcible illustrations of eminently sound moral and religious principles, but undeniably its general effect is rather flattening.

Was all this wealth of loving observation and imaginative rendering of nature and common life used merely to adorn moral generalities? Was the Jesus of the Gospels just an eminently sound and practical teacher, who patiently led simple

[5] *Gleichnisreden Jesu*, II, 1910, p. 481.

minds to appreciate the great enduring commonplaces of morals and religion? This is not the impression conveyed by the Gospels as a whole. There is one of His parabolic sayings which runs: "I have come to set fire to the earth, and how I wish it were already kindled!" Few parables are more difficult to interpret with precision; none perhaps is clearer in its main purport. Indeed any attempt to paraphrase its meaning is both less clear and less forcible than the saying as it stands. It is exactly the phrase we need to describe the volcanic energy of the meteoric career depicted in the Gospels. The teaching of Jesus is not the leisurely and patient exposition of a system by the founder of a school. It is related to a brief and tremendous crisis in which He is the principal figure and which indeed His appearance brought about.

Thus we should expect the parables to bear upon the actual and critical situation in which Jesus and His hearers stood; and when we ask after their application, we must look first, not to the field of general principles, but to the particular setting in which they were delivered. The task of the interpreter of the parables is to find out, if he can, the setting of a parable in the situation contemplated by the Gospels, and hence the application which would suggest itself to one who stood in that situation.[6]

We may first ask, how far the evangelists themselves help us to relate the parables to their setting. It might be thought that the place in which a parable comes in the order of the narrative would give a decisive clue. But in the first place, the evangelists sometimes give the same parable in different settings; and secondly, recent research has tended to show that the materials of the Gospels were at first transmitted in the form of independent units, the framework being supplied by the evangelists who wrote not less than a generation after the time of Jesus. While I think myself that this judgment needs qualification, and that more of the framework was traditional than some recent writers suppose,[7] yet it is clear

[6] See A. T. Cadoux, *op. cit.* We now have in J. Jeremias's *Die Gleichnisse Jesu* a work which carries this principle through consistently.

[7] See my article, "The Framework of the Gospel Narrative," in the *Expository Times*, vol. xliii, p. 396 sqq, reprinted in *New Testament Studies* (Manchester University Press 1953) pp. 1-11.

that we cannot without question assume that the setting in which we have a parable in its original setting in history. It is only where something in the parable itself seems to link it with some special phrase of the ministry that we dare press the precise connection. More often we shall have to be content with relating it to the situation as a whole.

Apart, however, from the setting of the parables in the narrative, the evangelists sometimes, though by no means always, give an indication of the intended application. These usually brief applications stand on a different footing from the elaborate allegorizations of the Sower, the Tares and the Net, and they deserve more attention. It is however, necessary to ask how far such applications can be regarded as original. The tendency of recent writers from Jülicher to Bultmann is to discount them all heavily. But it would be well not to go too far in this direction. To begin with, parables with applications (no less than parables without applications) occur in all our four main Gospel strata. While therefore any particular application may be the work of this or that evangelist, the primitive tradition underlying the variously differentiated traditions from which our Gospels are derived, was certainly acquainted with applied parables.

Moreover, in many cases the application shows by its form that it had an organic connection with the parable itself from the earliest stage that we can trace. Thus in the parable of the Two Houses the application is so interwoven with the story, in Matthew and Luke alike, that it could not be eliminated without rewriting the story completely. And observe that the application thus suggested is not general but particular. We have not a simple contrast between hearing and doing. The actual listeners to the words of Jesus then and there will be as foolish, if they do not follow them, as a builder who chooses a site on floodland, with no firm foundation.

Again, the parable of the Children in the Market-place is followed immediately by a passage which by its form shows that it is a part of the same tradition : —

" John came neither eating nor drinking, and you say, He is possessed.

The Son of Man came eating and drinking, and you say,
See, a glutton and a drinker,
A friend of publicans and sinners!"

I cannot bring myself to doubt that the earliest tradition contained this application of the parable to the people in their
attitude to Jesus and John. It is clear that any attempt to
work it out by way of an allegorical equivalence of terms
breaks down. You cannot say, Jesus and His disciples are
the piping children, John and his disciples the mourning
children; the picture does not fit. But the picture of petulant
children who quarrel about their games suggests the frivolous
captiousness of a generation who would not see that the
movement inaugurated by John and brought to such an unexpected pitch by Jesus was a crisis of the first magnitude,
but wasted their time in foolish carping at the asceticism of
the one, and the good-companionship of the other. They
fiddled while Rome was burning.

Thus there are cases where, without necessarily solving the
possibly unanswerable question whether we have the *ipsissima
verba* of Jesus, we may have confidence that the application
of the parable came down with the parable itself in the earliest
tradition, and therefore shows us at the least how the parable
was understood by those who stood near to the very situation
which had called it forth.

On the other hand there are grounds for suspecting that
in many cases the application was not a part of the earlier
tradition, but was supplied by the evangelist, or by his immediate authority, representing no doubt the current exegesis
in that part of the Church to which he belonged. It is noteworthy that sometimes a parable occurs without application
in one Gospel and is supplied with one in another, as for
example, the parable of the Lamp occurs in Mark and Luke
without any application, but in Matthew is followed by the
injunction, " In the same way your light must shine before men,
that they may see your good works, and glorify your Father
in heaven." Again, sometimes a parable occurs in two or more
Gospels with different and even inconsistent applications, as,
for example, the parable of the Savourless Salt. We must
suppose that Jesus intended some one definite application;

hence either one, or more probably both, of the applications are secondary.

Sometimes different applications are supplied even by the same evangelist. Thus to the very difficult parable of the Unjust Steward (Lk. xvi. 1-7) the evangelist has appended a whole series of " morals ": (i) " the sons of this age are more prudent in relation to their own time than the sons of light," (ii) " make friends by means of unrighteous wealth," (iii) " if you have not been honest with unrighteous wealth, who will entrust you with the true riches." We can almost see here notes for the three separate sermons on the parable as text.

It is possible that the clause with which the parable itself appears to close was the application in the earliest form of tradition. The reporter of the parable added, " The Lord (Jesus) commended the unjust steward because he had acted prudently." In that case we can relate the parable to its setting in this way. The story tells of a man suddenly faced with a crisis which may mean utter ruin to him, realizing the seriousness of his position, he does some strenuous thinking, and finds out a drastic means of coping with the situation. The hearers are invited to make the judgment: this man, scoundrel as he was, at least had the merit of taking a realistic and practical view of a crisis. They would then reflect that, as Jesus was constantly urging, they themselves stood before a momentous crisis. Surely, He would have them conclude, it was only common sense to think strenuously and act boldly to meet the crisis. This seems to me to be the most probable application of the parable, and in that case, the evangelist's further comment, " The sons of this age are more prudent than the sons of light," is apt enough.

On the other hand it is possible that the clause, " The lord commended the unjust steward " is actually part of the parable. The " Lord " is then the character in the story, the defrauded master, and the statement that he commended his fraudulent steward is so palpably absurd that it provokes the hearers to deny it vigorously. In fact it is a strong way of putting the question, " What think ye?" In that case we must relate the story to its setting in this way. Here is a man who feathered his nest by sharp practice, and actually expected to be commended for it! Who then, among the hearers, or among people known to them, were acting in that way? Possibly the Sadducaic priesthood, who made a merit of keeping in with the Romans by concessions which they had no right to make.[8] Possibly the Pharisees, who by a little easy alms giving sought to make of their ill-gotten riches a means of winning the divine favour.[9] It is clear that in this case there was no certain clue to the application of the parable even when it reached the evangelist Luke, and that he was given a variety of current interpretations.

I shall presently try to point out certain changes in the historical situation which have led to the re-application of parables in senses not originally intended. In any such case we must carefully scrutinize the parable itself, and attempt to relate it to the original situation, so far as we can re-construct it. From this will follow the conclusion regarding its original meaning and application, which may be guided by the following principles: (i) The clue must be found, not in ideas which developed only with the experience of the early Church, but in such ideas as may be supposed to have been in the minds of the hearers of Jesus during His ministry. Our best guide to such ideas will often be the Old Testament, with which they may be presumed to have been familiar. Thus the images of a vineyard, a fig-tree, harvest, a feast, and others, had associations which could escape no one brought up on the Old Testament.[10] (ii) The meaning which we attribute to the parable must be congruous with the interpretation of His own ministry offered by Jesus in explicit and unambiguous sayings, so far as such sayings are known to us; and in any case it must be such as to fit the general view of His teaching to which a study of the non-parabolic sayings leads. A pre-liminary task, therefore, will be to define, so far as we can, the general orientation of the teaching of Jesus.

Among the parables reported in the Gospels a certain number are introduced with some form of words such as " The King-dom of God is like . . ." This introductory formula may be regarded as giving the " application " of these parables.

[8] So A. T. Cadoux, *The Parables of Jesus*, p. 135.
[9] So Henri Clavier in *Etudes Théologiques et Religieuses* 1929, p. 333.
[10] Emphasis is laid upon this point in Hoskyns and Davey, *The Riddle of the New Testament*, pp. 177 sqq.

In Mark two parables are so introduced, those of the Seed Growing Secretly and of the Mustard Seed. In Luke again there are two, the Mustard Seed and the Leaven. As these two also occur in Matthew with the like introduction, we may take it that they stood in the common source (" Q ") of the first and third Gospels. In Matthew there are eight other parables introduced in this way. One of them, the Great Feast is given in a different form in Luke, where it is not explicitly applied to the Kingdom of God. The others are the parables of the Tares, the Hid Treasure, the Costly Pearl, the Drag-net the Unforgiving Servant,[11] the Labourers in the Vineyard, and the Ten Virgins. It appears that this form of introduction was a favourite one with the First Evangelist, and it may well be that he has made use of it in some cases where it was absent from the earlier tradition. As we have seen, the evangelists use a certain freedom in applying parables. But he has not used it indiscriminately, for the majority of the parables which he reports have no such introduction.

At any rate we have three parables, those of the Seed Growing Secretly, the Mustard Seed and the Leaven, in which the reference to the Kingdom of God is attested by one or other of our earlier sources, and in one case, by both of them (the strongest form of attestation which our Gospels can provide). It is therefore certain that Jesus did make use of parables to illustrate what Mark calls " the mystery of the Kingdom of God " (iv. 11). I shall try to show that not only the parables which are explicitly referred to the Kingdom of God, but many others do in fact bear upon this idea, and that a study of them throws important light upon its meaning.

---

[11] I have failed to find any specific link between this parable (Mt. xviii. 23-35) and the idea of the Kingdom of God, apart from the general notion of judgment. I suspect that in this case the formula has become conventional. In all other cases it does seem to have real point.

Chapter II

THE KINGDOM OF GOD

The two expressions, "The Kingdom of God" and "The Kingdom of Heaven," the latter of which is peculiar to the First Gospel, are synonymous, the term "heaven" being common in Jewish usage as a reverential periphrasis for the divine name. The term "kingdom" is in English somewhat ambiguous, but it naturally suggests a territory or a community governed by a king. The Greek term βασιλεία which it translates is also ambiguous. But there can be no doubt that the expression before us represents an Aramaic phrase well-established in Jewish usage, "The *malkuth* of Heaven." *Malkuth*, like other substantives of the same formation, is properly an abstract noun, meaning "kingship," "kingly rule," "reign" or "sovereignty." The expression "the *malkuth* of God" connotes the fact that God reigns as King.[1] In sense, though not in grammatical form, the substantive conception in the phrase "the Kingdom of God" is the idea of God, and the term "kingdom" indicates that specific aspect, attribute or activity of God, in which He is revealed as King or Sovereign Lord of His people, or of the universe which He created.[2]

[1] Thus Exod. xv. 18, "The Lord shall reign for ever and ever," is paraphrased in the Targum of Onkelos, "His *malkuth* stands for ever and ever." (Dalman, *Worte Jesu*, 1898, p. 79.) "There can be no doubt," says Dalman, "that in the O.T. as in Jewish literature, *malkuth* as related to God always means 'kingly rule' and never 'kingdom'." It seems best, however, to retain the traditional expression, "The Kingdom of God," bearing in mind that the word "kingdom" carries in this case the sense of "kingly rule."

[2] The question may be raised whether the frequent modern use of the term "The Kingdom," as an abbreviation for the full phrase found in the Gospels, does not betray an unconscious presumption that the primary idea is that of an ordered society, which may be a kingdom of justice, or of brotherhood, or the like, though since we look to God for help to "bring in" or "build" such a kingdom, we may call it the Kingdom of God. In a book by the American labour leader Bouck White, *The Call of the Carpenter*, written to claim Jesus as a "proletarian" prophet, the author says, ingenuously enough, "The modern reader can perhaps grasp the 'Kingdom of Heaven' as Jesus used it—

29

In Jewish usage contemporary with the Gospels we may distinguish two main ways in which the Kingdom of God is spoken of.

First, God is King of His people Israel, and His kingly rule is effective in so far as Israel is obedient to the divine will as revealed in the Torah. To submit oneself unquestioningly to the Law is "to take upon oneself the *malkuth* of heaven."[3] In this sense "The Kingdom of God" is a present fact.

But in another sense "The Kingdom of God" is something yet to be revealed. God is more than King of Israel; He is King of all the world. But the world does not recognize Him as King. His own people is in fact subject to secular powers, which in the present age are permitted to exercise *malkuth*. Israel, however, looks forward to the day when 'The saints of the Most High shall take the kingdom,'[4] and so the kingship of God will become effective over the whole world. It is with this intention that pious Jews in the first century prayed (as they still pray), "May He establish His Kingdom during your life and during your days, and during the life of all the house of Israel."[5] In this sense "The Kingdom of God" is a hope for the future. It is itself the *eschaton*, or "ultimate," with which "eschatology" is concerned.

As such, the idea is capable of entering into association with various views of the "good time coming" as set forth in prophecy and apocalyptic. The hope may be a temporal and

---

so far as a single phrase can embody it—by substituting for it in every case another term, 'The Kingdom of self-respect.'" It is noteworthy that when a Jew spoke of "the kingdom" without qualification, he meant the secular government; e.g. *Pirqe Aboth*, iii, 7. "Everyone who receives upon him the yoke of Torah, they remove from him the yoke of the kingdom and the yoke of worldly occupation." Whatever social applications may be given to the teaching of Jesus, the essentially religious idea of God reigning in the lives of men and in human society lies at the bottom of it all.

[3] See passages cited in Dalman, *Worte Jesu*, pp. 79-80.
[4] Dan, vii. 18.
[5] *Kaddish* in the Jewish *Authorized Daily Prayer-Book*, translated by S. Singer, authorized by the Chief Rabbi, and published by Eyre and Spottiswoode, 1908, p. 86.

political one. Thus in the Eighteen Benedictions[6] we have the prayer.

> " Bring back our judges as at first, and our rulers as afore-times, and be Thou King over us, O Lord, thou alone."

On the other hand, it may be associated with the final and absolute state of bliss in a transcendant order, as in the *Assumption of Moses,* ch. x:

> " And then His Kingdom shall appear throughout all His creation,
> And then Satan shall be no more,
> And sorrow shall depart with him . . .
> For the Heavenly One will arise from His royal throne,
> And He will go forth from His holy habitation
> With indignation and wrath on account of His sons . . .
> For the Most High will arise, the Eternal God alone,
> And He will appear to punish the Gentiles,
> And He will destroy all idols.
> And thou, Israel, shalt be happy, . . .
> And God will exalt thee,
> And He will cause thee to approach to the heaven of the stars."[7]

Where a personal Messiah is looked for, the kingly rule of God is thought of as exercised by the Messiah, whether He is a human prince of the house of David, or a supernatural personage. Thus in the *Apocalypse of Baruch* ch. lxxiii:

> " And it shall come to pass.
> When He (the Messiah) has brought low everything that is in the world.
> And has sat down in peace for the age on the throne of His kingdom.
> That joy shall then be revealed,
> And rest shall appear,"[8]

[6] *Shemoneh Esre*; text in Dalman, *Worte Jesu,* pp. 299-301, after Schechter in *Jewish Quarterly Review,* 1898, pp. 564-659.
[7] Translation by Charles in *Apocrypha and Pseudepigrapha.*
[8] Translation by Charles in *op. cit.*

In all these forms of belief the common underlying idea is that of God's sovereign power becoming manifestly effective in the world of human experience. When it pleases God to " reveal " or to " set up " His kingly rule, then there will be judgment on all the wrong that is in the world, victory over all powers of evil and, for those who have accepted His sovereignty, deliverance and a blessed life in communion with Him.[9]

In considering the meaning of " The Kingdom of God " in the Gospels, we shall do well to be guided by the results of source-criticism. It would now be generally agreed (a) that

[9] Rudolph Otto in his important book, *Reich Gottes und Menschensohn* (1934), to which I am greatly indebted, pp. 9 sqq., derives the " eschatological " idea of the Kingdom of God from Zoroastrian, and ultimately from primitive Aryan, religious conceptions. Iranian influence upon Judaism is undeniable, and it was to be expected, since the Jews were for some two centuries subjects of the Persian Empire. But there are certain facts recorded by Otto himself which lead one to doubt whether that influence has really been determinative of the idea of the Kingdom of God. In Iranian writings, apparently, the regular term is *chshathra,* " the Kingdom " or *chshathra varya,* " the kingdom of choice or desire," and *chshathra,* though it may mean " kingly rule," as often means " kingdom " in the strict sense (" Herrschaftsgebiet "). In Judaism, on the other hand, it is always " the kingship *of* God (*Heaven*)." As a matter of fact, the apocalypses, in which the influence of Iranian eschatology is most marked, avoid the use of the phrase " The Kingdom of God," with rare exceptions. On the other hand, the idea of God as king is characteristic of Semitic religion. The god is king of his tribe; its leader in war, its judge in peace, the source of its law as well as the object of its worship. In Israel this naïve belief in the kingship of Jehovah was complicated by the emergence of ethical monotheism in the teaching of the prophets. On the one hand, Jehovah is the King of Israel; on the other hand, He is the only God, and His will is universal righteousness. His Kingship therefore extends over the whole earth, and where He is King righteousness prevails. But, in fact, the people whose King was the Lord came to be subject to the " unrighteous ", who worshipped other gods. On the naïve view, this ought to mean that Jehovah is subject to these other gods. But the higher faith stoutly maintained, in the face of all discouragement, that " the Most High ruleth in the kingdom of men, and giveth it to whomsoever he will " (Dan. iv. 17). Sooner or later He will reveal His sovereignty. He will be King of all the world, not only *de jure* but *de facto* : " the saints of the Most High shall take the kingdom " (Dan. vii. 18). Thus the eschatological idea of the Kingdom of God seems to arise naturally from primitive Hebrew conceptions, under the influence of prophetic teaching and of outward events.

the material which appears in all three Synoptic Gospels lies before us (broadly speaking) in its earliest form in Mark; (b) that where Matthew and Luke agree independently of Mark, they are following a second source of some kind. Much of their common material seems to have been contained in a single document, but some of it may have been handed down in floating tradition. The symbol 'Q' is often used to denote the supposed lost document; but as its reconstruction is problematical, it seems best to use this symbol for that *stratum* of the First and Third Gospels in which they agree together but do not seem to depend on Mark as a source. In using the Gospels as documents for the life and teaching of Jesus it is not necessary to decide whether a given passage did or did not form part of a written document before it entered into our Gospels. In any case, if Matthew and Luke show any striking measure of agreement, and if this agreement cannot be accounted for by their common use of Mark, then the material in question did in any case belong to a tradition, substantially earlier than any date we can assign to the completed Gospels, and that is all we really need to know.

As for the remaining portions of the First and Third Gospels, they come from sources of which we can say little. If the once widely accepted theory of B. H. Streeter is right, we have to allow for four relatively primitive sources, those represented by Mark, 'Q' and the peculiar portions of Matthew and Luke respectively. But although we may suspect that the two latter were possibly as old as Mark or 'Q', we can never know whether a given passage in Matthew or Luke was drawn directly from the early sources, or whether it represents a later development. We know from their treatment of Mark that the other synoptists used their sources with some freedom. Nor, if it be true (as I think it probably is) that behind the Third Gospel lies a 'proto-Luke' which might be as early as Mark, are we entitled to give the same weight to this hypothetical document as we give to the Second Gospel; because (a) we do not know what amount of revision 'proto-Luke' underwent in being incorporated in the Third Gospel, and (b) the peculiarly Lucan material, on its merits, seems in places almost demonstrably secondary to Mark, even though in some places it may be thought to have preserved a more primitive tradition.

We are therefore left with Mark and 'Q' as primary sources, and I do not think criticism has yet provided us with any better *organon* for approximating to the original tradition of the words and works of Jesus than is supplied by a careful study and comparison of these two.[10] No one supposes that either of them is infallible. But they serve to correct, confirm and supplement one another,[11] and their agreement in some important points gives us confidence that we are in touch with the tradition at a very early stage indeed, before the two lines of transmission which culminated in Mark (at Rome) and 'Q' (in Palestine or Syria (?)), began to diverge.

In dealing therefore with the complicated question of the Kingdom of God, we shall not only be saving time by leaving out of account (with few exceptions) those parts of Matthew and Luke which have no parallel in other Gospels, but we shall also be dealing with material which has the best claim to bring us in touch with the earliest tradition accessible to us at all.

The twofold Jewish usage of the expression " The Kingdom of God " is reflected in the teaching of Jesus as recorded in the earliest traditions.

The Rabbinic expression " to take upon oneself the *malkuth* of heaven " finds a parallel in the saying of Mk. x. 15: " Whoever does not *receive the Kingdom of God* as a little child will never enter into it." The Rabbis meant by this the scrupulous observance of the Torah. Jesus was evidently under-

[10] The school of *Formgeschichte* (form-criticism) seeks to go behind our written sources to the oral tradition. It often illuminates the development of the tradition, and I have not been unmindful of its methods in what follows. But I do not think it has yet provided us with a trustworthy criterion for the historical value of the reports in the Gospels. And we must always bear in mind that any deeper analysis on Mark and " Q " must be speculative in a sense in which the determination of the proximate sources of the Gospels is not speculative but demonstrative.

[11] I assume that Mark and " Q " are independent of one another. The attempts to show that Mark depends on " Q ", and that " Q " depends on Mark, cancel out, and neither has carried conviction.

stood to contrast the way of the "little child," or the "babe" (Mt. xi. 25; Lk. x. 21)[12] with the way of the "wise and prudent."[13] For him, to accept the sovereignty of God is something other than scrupulous observance of the Torah.[14]

Again, the Jewish prayer, "May He establish His Kingdom during your life and during your days," finds a parallel in the central petition of the Lord's prayer, "Thy Kingdom come." The apocalyptic predictions of a future, and final, manifestation of the sovereign power of God are echoed (though, as we shall see, with a difference) in such sayings as Mk. ix. 1, "There are some of those who stand here who will never taste death until they have seen that the Kingdom of God has come with power"; Mt. viii. 11, "Many will come from east and west, and sit at meat with Abraham, Isaac and Jacob in the Kingdom of God." Like some of the apocalyptists, it would appear that Jesus placed the ultimate Kingdom of God in an order beyond space and time, where the blessed dead live for ever "like the angels" (Mk. xii. 25). Accordingly, the expression "The Kingdom of God" is used in Mk. ix. 43-47, x. 17, 24, 25, alternately with "life" or "eternal life". The latter expression is an equivalent for the Rabbinic term "the life of the Age to Come," which is in our Jewish sources a far more usual expression than "the Kingdom of God" for the great object of hope, the *eschaton*.

So far, the use of the expression "The Kingdom of God" in the Gospels falls well within the framework of contemporary Jewish usage. The Kingdom of God may be "accepted" here and now, and its blessings will be enjoyed in the end by those who have fulfilled the necessary conditions.

But there are other sayings which do not fall within this

---

[12] In Mt. xi. 29, Jesus speaks of His "yoke," no doubt in contrast with "the yoke of Torah," which was also spoken of as "the yoke of the *malkuth* of heaven."

[13] The "disciples of the wise" are in the Talmud the members of the Rabbinic school of Torah.

[14] The precept "Seek the Kingdom of God" (which is probably the original form of the "Q" saying in Mt. vi. 33; Lk. xii. 31) is perhaps best brought under this heading. Any reference to the "eschatological" kingdom of God is difficult to work out. To "seek the Kingdom of God" is to make the doing of His will the supreme aim. Cf. Mk. iii. 35.

framework. "The Kingdom of God has come upon you" (Mt. xii. 28 = Lk. xi. 20).[15] Here the Kingdom of God is a fact of present experience, but not in the sense which we have recognized in Jewish usage. Any Jewish teacher might have said, "If you repent and pledge yourself to the observance of Torah, then you have taken upon yourselves the Kingdom of God." But Jesus says, "If I, by the finger of God, cast out demons, then the Kingdom of God has come upon you." Something has happened, which has not happened before, and which means that the sovereign power of God has come into effective operation. It is not a matter of having God for your King in the sense that you obey His commandments: it is a matter of being confronted with the power of God at work in the world. In other words, the "eschatological" Kingdom of God is proclaimed as a present fact, which men must recognize, whether by their actions they accept or reject it.

The same sense seems to be intended by the formula in which Mark sums up the preaching of Jesus in Galilee (Mk. i. 14-15); "The time has reached fulfilment, and the Kingdom of God had drawn near. Repent and believe the Gospel." On the face of it this might mean either that the Kingdom of God is near in point of time, i.e. that it will soon come; or that (in spatial metaphor, cf. Mk. xii. 34) it is within reach. But in the LXX ἐγγίζειν is sometimes used (chiefly in past tenses) to translate the Hebrew verb *nagá* and the Aramaic verb *m'ta*, both of which mean "to reach," "to arrive". The same two verbs are also translated by the verb φθάνειν, which is used in Mt. xii. 28, Lk. xi. 20. It would appear therefore that no difference of meaning is intended

---

[15] Ἔφθασεν ἐφ' ὑμᾶς ἡ βασιλεία τοῦ θεοῦ. The verb φθάνειν in classical Greek has the sense, "to anticipate" someone, to get before him, and so to be there before he knows. But in Hellenistic Greek it is used, especially in the aorist, to denote the fact that a person has actually arrived at his goal. This usage is preserved in modern Greek. If you call a waiter, I am told, he will say, as he bustles up, "ἔφθασα, κύριε!" Thus ἔφθασεν ἡ βασιλεία τοῦ θεοῦ expresses in the most vivid and forcible way the fact that the Kingdom of God has actually arrived. Prof. Millar Burrows, of Yale, pointed out to me that ἔφθασεν ἐφ' ὑμᾶς ἡ βασιλεία τοῦ θεοῦ sounds like an echo of Dan. vii. 22 (as rendered by Theodotion) ἔφθασεν ὁ καιρός, καὶ τὴν βασιλείαν ἔσχον οἱ ἅγιοι.

between ἔφθασεν ἐφ' ὑμᾶς ἡ βασιλεία τοῦ θεοῦ and ἤγγικεν ἡ βασιλεία τοῦ θεοῦ. Both imply the " arrival " of the Kingdom. With an eye on the presumed Aramaic original, we should translate both: " The Kingdom of God has come." And again we observe that the coming of the Kingdom of God is not represented as something dependent on the attitude of men. It is an historical happening, to which men should respond by repentance, but whether they repent or not, it is there. This is made quite clear in the Lucan form of the Charge to Missionaries: " Say to them, ' The Kingdom of God has come upon you ' (ἤγγικεν ἐφ' ὑμᾶς, cf. ἔφθασεν ἐφ' ὑμᾶς, Mt. xii. 28, Lk. xi. 20). And if you enter any city and they do not receive you, go into their streets and say, ' Even the dust which sticks to our feet from your city we wipe off for you; but all the same, be sure that the Kingdom of God has come (ἤγγικεν) ' " (Lk. x. 9-11).[16]

It is instructive to compare such an apocalyptic passage as the *Testament of Dan,* v. 31-vi. 4: " The Lord will be in the midst of her, and the Holy One of Israel reigning from her . . . for he knows that on the day when Israel is converted, the kingdom of the Enemy will be brought to an end." In the " Q " context from which the words " The Kingdom of God has come upon you " have been quoted, the exorcisms performed by Jesus are treated as a sign that the kingdom of Satan has been overcome. As in the *Testament of Dan,* this is equivalent to the coming of the Kingdom of God. But here the coming has not waited until Israel should repent. In some way the Kingdom of God has come with Jesus Himself[17] and that Kingdom is proclaimed, " whether they will hear or whether they will forbear," as Ezekiel might have said. It is an act of God's grace to reveal His Kingdom to an unrepentant generation, that they may be provoked to repentance.

There are other passages in our oldest Gospel sources which

[16] For a fuller statement of the evidence for the meaning of ἔφθασεν and ἤγγικεν, see my article " The Kingdom of God has come " in *Expository Times,* vol. xlviii, no. 3, pp. 138-141.

[17] Otto, *op cit.,* p. 80, is, I think, right, " Nicht Jesus ' bringt ' das Reich—eine Vorstellung, die Jesu selber ganz fremd ist—sondern das Reich bringt ihn mit." Jesus is " sent " by the Father, who in sending Him, causes His Kingdom to come.

help to make it clear that Jesus intended to proclaim the Kingdom of God not as something to come in the near future, but as a matter of present experience. " Blessed are the eyes that see what you see; for I tell you that many prophets and kings wished to see what you see, and did not see it, and to hear what you hear and did not hear it " (Lk. x. 23-24, and with insignificant variations, Mt. xiii. 16-17). That which prophets and kings (such as David the psalmist, and Solomon, to whom the Messianic " Psalms of Solomon " were attributed), desired, is naturally to be understood as the final assertion of God's sovereignty in the world, the coming of " the Kingdom of God." This it is that the disciples of Jesus " see and hear." Again, " The queen of the South will rise up in the judgment with this generation, and condemn it; because she came from the ends of the earth to hear the wisdom of Solomon, and behold something greater[18] than Solomon is here. The men of Nineveh will stand up in the judgment with this generation and condemn it; because they repented at the preaching of Jonah, and behold something greater than Jonah is here " (Lk. xi. 31-32 = Mt. xii. 41-42). What is this " something greater " than Jonah the prophet and Solomon the wise king? Surely it is that which prophets and kings desired to see, the coming of the Kingdom of God.

The same idea seems to be intended in the series of sayings about John the Baptist given, from a common source, in Mt. xi. 2-11 and Lk. vii. 18-30. In answer to John's question, " Are you the Coming One, or are we to expect another?" Jesus points to the phenomena of His own ministry in terms which clearly allude to prophecies of the " good time coming." The implication is that the time of fulfilment has come: that which the prophets desired to see is now matter of present experience. John is himself not merely one of the prophets, but greater than any prophet, because he is the Messenger of whom the prophets spoke, who should immediately precede the great divine event, the coming of the Kingdom of God. The implication is clear: John has played his destined part, and the Kingdom of God has come. And as the disciples of Jesus are more privileged than prophets

---

[18] πλεῖον, the neuter adjective; not " a greater than Solomon ", which would require the masculine.

and kings who desired the coming of the Kingdom of God, because they " see and hear " the tokens of its presence, so they are " greater " than John the Baptist because they are " within the Kingdom of God "[19] which he had heralded. Matthew adds here a saying which is given in a different form in Lk. xvi. 16. The two forms are as follows:

MATTHEW	LUKE
" From the days of John the Baptist until now the Kingdom of heaven is forced and men of force make prey of it. For all the prophets and the law prophesied until John."	" The law and the prophets were until John: from that time on the Kingdom of God is proclaimed and everyone forces his way into it."

The original form of the saying, and its precise meaning, are exceedingly difficult to determine; but it seems clear that a contrast is drawn between the past and the present. John the Baptist marks the dividing line: before him, the law and the prophets; after him, the Kingdom of God.[20] In Luke at least it is clear that any interim period is excluded. In Matthew it is possible that the additional words " until now " (ἕως ἄρτι) are intended to allow for such an interim period between the baptism of John and the coming of the Kingdom of God—the period, namely, of our Lord's earthly ministry.

[19] Or, in other words, " theirs is the Kingdom of God " (Mt. v. 3; Lk. vi. 20; cf. Mk. x. 14). The variety of expression does not carry with it different conceptions of the Kingdom, as a realm which one can enter in the one case and a treasure one can possess in the other (cf. Mk. x. 15; Mt. xiii. 44-46). Both are ways of saying that the coming of the Kingdom of God is realized in experience.

[20] According to Mt. iii. 2, John also said ἤγγικεν ἡ βασιλεία τῶν οὐρανῶν. But Matthew cannot be trusted to distinguish between words of John and words of Jesus. In vii. 19 he has intruded into a " Q " passage the words πᾶν δένδρον μὴ ποιοῦν καρπὸν καλὸν ἐκκόπτεται καὶ εἰς πῦρ βάλλεται, which belong to the " Q " report of the teaching of the Baptist (Mt. iii. 10 = Lk. iii. 9, word for word); and in xxiii. 33 he has put into the mouth of Jesus the words γεννήματα ἐχιδνῶν, πῶς φύγητε ἀπὸ τῆς κρίσεως τῆς γεέννης, which are not given by any other authority as words of Jesus, but are closely similar to the words given in " Q " to John the Baptist (Mt. iii. 7 = Lk. iii. 7). Conversely as none of our other evangelists suggest that John used the words which Matthew attributes to him in iii. 2, we must take it that he has here mistakenly attributed words of Jesus to the Baptist. See also Otto, op. cit., pp. 58-63.

Yet even for Matthew the Kingdom of God must have been in some sense a present reality "from the days of John the Baptist until" the moment of speaking, that is to say, throughout the ministry of Jesus, since it is said to be the object of human "force" (whatever that may mean). In any case the *general* implication of the whole passage, Mt. xi. 4-19 with its Lucan parallels seems to me to be unmistakable: the old order closed with the ministry of John; the new begins with the ministry of Jesus.

These passages, the most explicit of their kind, are sufficient to show that in the earliest tradition Jesus was understood to have proclaimed that the Kingdom of God, the hope of many generations, had at last come. It is not merely imminent; it is here. In whatever way this is to be reconciled with other passages in which the coming of the Kingdom of God is still an object of hope and prayer, as it is in Jewish thought, we must do justice to the plain meaning of the passages we have just considered. That school of interpretation which professed to find the key to the teaching of Jesus in "thorough-going eschatology" ("consequente Eschatologie"), was really proposing a compromise. In the presence of one set of sayings which appeared to contemplate the coming of the Kingdom of God as future, and another set which appeared to contemplate it as already present, they offered an interpretation which represented it as coming very, very soon. But this is no solution. Whatever we make of them, the sayings which declare the Kingdom of God to have come are explicit and unequivocal. They are moreover the most characteristic and distinctive of the Gospel sayings on the subject. They have no parallel in Jewish teaching or prayers of the period. If therefore we are seeking the *differentia* of the teaching of Jesus upon the Kingdom of God, it is here that it must be found.[21]

This declaration that the Kingdom of God has already come necessarily dislocates the whole eschatological scheme in which its expected coming closes the long vista of the future. The

[21] Among recent writers the one who does fullest justice to this idea is Rudolf Otto. His phrase for it is "der Schonanbruch des Reiches Gottes." I cannot see how anyone, after reading *Reich Gottes und Menschensohn*, pp. 51-73, could ever be content with interpretations which water down the meaning of these great sayings into a mere expectation that the Kingdom of God would come very soon.

eschaton has moved from the future to the present, from the sphere of expectation into that of realized experience. It is therefore unsafe to assume that the content of the idea, " The Kingdom of God," as Jesus meant it, may be filled in from the speculations of apocalyptic writers. They were referring to something in the future, which could be conceived only in terms of fantasy. He was speaking of that which, in one aspect at least, was an object of experience.

The common idea, as we have seen, underlying all uses of the term " The Kingdom of God " is that of the manifest and effective assertion of the divine sovereignty against all the evil of the world. In what sense, then, did Jesus declare that the Kingdom of God was present? Our answer must at least begin with His own answer to John : " The blind see, the lame walk, the lepers are cleansed, the deaf hear, the dead are raised, the poor have the Gospel preached to them." In the ministry of Jesus Himself the divine power is released in effective conflict with evil. " If I by the finger of God cast out demons, then the Kingdom of God has come upon you." When the Fourth Evangelist presents the works of healing as " signs " of the coming of " eternal life " to men, he is rightly interpreting these sayings in our earliest sources. For eternal life is the ultimate issue of the coming of the Kingdom of God, and this coming is manifested in the series of historical events which unfolds itself in the ministry of Jesus.

Here then is the fixed point from which our interpretation of the teaching regarding the Kingdom of God must start. It represents the ministry of Jesus as " realized eschatology," that is to say, as the impact upon this world of the " powers of the world to come " in a series of events, unprecedented and unrepeatable, now in actual process.

Nevertheless, the teaching of Jesus, as recorded in the Gospels, has reference to the future as well as to the present. We must enquire what is the relation of this predictive element in His teaching to the proclamation of the Kingdom of God as present.

It is no doubt possible to take the view that the predictions which we find in the Gospels are no more than a reflection of the experience of the early Church within which the tradition was formed. It is certain at least that some of them have been coloured by this experience. But we know that Jesus was widely regarded as a prophet, and prediction was a part of the traditional rôle of a prophet. Moreover, there seem to be traces (as we shall see) of predictions attributed to Him which were not in fact fulfilled, and therefore cannot be regarded as *vaticinia ex eventu*. We may therefore take it to be probable that He did on occasion utter predictions.

Some of these, as we have them in the Gospels, seem to refer plainly (in the manner of the classical prophets) to forthcoming historical events; others resemble the visionary forecast of the apocalypses, referring to events of a wholly supernatural order. In our Gospels these two types of prediction are mixed together, and to disentangle them is no easy task. Nevertheless the attempt must be made. We shall do well to depend mainly on the two earliest sources, Mark, and the common source, or strain of tradition, underlying Matthew and Luke (" Q "), and to check the one by the other. And here our task is the more difficult, because the most considerable predictive discourse in Mark, the " Little Apocalypse " of Mk. xiii, lies under the suspicion of being a secondary composition,[22] though it no doubt incorporates genuine sayings

[22] If, as Torrey and Bacon have argued, interest in the Danielic prediction of the " abomination of desolation " was revived by Caligula's unsuccessful attempt to desecrate the temple in A.D. 40, we have a *terminus post quem* for Mk. xiii. 14. The same idea of a horrible sacrilege in the temple is found in the apocalypse of II Thess. ii. 3-11 (probably A.D. 50). Further, down to xiii. 13, we seem to have references to the historical situation in the fifties or perhaps the early sixties: the rise of Messianic pretenders, wars and rumours of wars (the Parthian peril), earthquakes and famines, the citation of Christians before Jewish and provincial courts, and their growing isolation and unpopularity in society. The readers are warned that these events (which they are experiencing) are *not* " the End ". But we miss clear references to events after A.D. 64—the Neronian persecution (?), the Roman invasion of Judæa, the capture of Jerusalem and the burning of the temple. Instead of these notorious historical events we have a prediction of a horrible sacrilege in the temple, which in fact did not happen, followed immediately by the final tribulation and the collapse of the universe. On the principles usually followed in dating apocalypses, the inference would be that the " Little Apocalypse " belongs somewhere about the year 60. Whether it was composed by the evangelist, or taken over by him, and in the latter case, how far he worked over it, it is impossible to say. It may be that a short

of Jesus. We cannot use it as it stands for evidence of His own forecast of the future. Its various component parts must be examined separately, and compared with our other primary course.

We enquire, therefore, what, on the testimony of the best sources to which we have access, did Jesus predict?

In the first place, it is difficult to point to any precise prediction of the coming of the Kingdom of God. There is no saying of the unequivocal form, " The Kingdom of God will come," to balance the statement, " The Kingdom of God has come," The nearest thing to such a saying in our earliest sources is Mk. ix. 1: "There are some of those standing here who will not taste death until they have seen that the Kingdom of God has come with power."[28] The meaning appears to be that some of those who heard Jesus speak would before their death awake to the fact that the Kingdom of God had come. The only open question is whether Jesus meant that the Kingdom had already, in His ministry, come " with power," and that His hearers would afterwards recognize the fact, or whether He intended to distinguish its partial coming at the moment of speaking from some subsequent

---

apocalypse, similar to that which underlies II Thess. ii. 3-11, circulated shortly after A.D. 40, and that the evangelist brought it up to date.

[28] Ἕως αν ιδωσιν τήν βασιλείαν τοῦ θεοῦ ἐληλυθυῖαν ἐν δυνάμει. The meaning is either, "until they see the Kingdom of God as something that has already come," or else (the participle being used as the equivalent of the accusative and infinitive with verbs *dicendi et sentiendi*) "until they see that the Kingdom of God has come" (if indeed the two constructions are really different). In any case the perfect participle indicates an action already complete from the standpoint of the subject of the main verb. (See further the article cited above, *Expository Times*, vol. xlviii, no. 3, pp. 141-142.) The bystanders are not promised that they shall see the Kingdom of God *coming,* but that they shall come to see that the Kingdom of God *has already come,* at some point before they became aware of it. The Aramaic language is equally capable of this distinction. The old Syriac renders *nechzun malkutha d' alaha d' athya,* literally, "they shall see the Kingdom of God which is coming"; the Peshitta, correctly, *nechzun malkutha d' alaha d' etha,* "they shall see the Kingdom of God which has come" (or "that it has come").

coming "with power." Our answer to this question will depend on our interpretation of other passages.[24]

Next we have the saying in Mt. viii. 11 (with its parallel in Lk. xiii. 28-29): "Many will come from east and west and sit at meat with Abraham, Isaac and Jacob in the Kingdom of God." As we have seen, this is congruous with the apocalyptic idea of the "life of the Age to Come," presented under the similitude of a feast with the blessed dead. But it is not said that the Kingdom in which the patriarchs feast is yet to come. What has not yet happened, but will happen, is that many who are not yet "in the Kingdom of God," in its earthly manifestation, will enjoy its ultimate fulfilment in a world beyond this. The saying does not answer the question whether or not Jesus expected any further "coming" of the Kingdom of God beyond that which was already taking place in His own ministry. It may be that the patriarchs are thought of as living "in the Kingdom of God,"[25] in the world beyond this, where God's Kingdom does not "come," but is eternally present. That God is King in heaven from all eternity is a postulate of Jewish theology. The new thing is that His Kingdom shall be revealed on earth. This according to the teaching of Jesus has already happened. The saying before us does not conflict with that statement. It would however be susceptible of the meaning that at some date in the future the present earthly manifestation of the Kingdom of God will

[24] It may be observed that the use of the phrase "with power" recalls the Christological formula in Rom. i. 3-4; "His Son, who was born of the seed of David according to the flesh, who was appointed Son of God with power according to the Spirit of holiness from the time (or, ' on the ground ') of the resurrection of the dead." Here the resurrection marks the transition from the earlier phase of Christ's work to the phase "with power." The Christological formula is probably not Pauline in origin, but appears to represent a confession known at Rome (see my commentary on *Romans* in the Moffatt Commentary). The Gospel according to Mark belongs to Rome. It is a likely conjecture that the idea associated with the phrase "with power" is the same in both documents. Whether in both it was ultimately derived from an authentic word of Jesus is a question to which there can be no certain answer, but even if the precise phrase should be regarded as unoriginal, that does not necessarily decide the question whether or not it substantially agrees with the thought of Jesus.

[25] Jesus said that the patriarchs were alive (and not in some state of suspended existence, awaiting a resurrection), since God is their God and He is not a God of the dead but of the living (Mk. xii 26-27).

yield to a purely transcendent order in which it will be absolute.

The same background of ideas lies behind the saying at the Last Supper, Mk. xiv. 25; "I will never again drink of the fruit of the vine until that day when I drink it new in the Kingdom of God."[26] The figure of the heavenly feast determines the symbolism. Jesus is about to die. He will never again partake of wine at any earthly meal, but he will drink wine in a new sort, "in the Kingdom of God." The form of expression suggests something of a pause or interval before this comes about. Are we to think of the Kingdom of God here as something yet to come? If so, it is not to come in this world, for the "new wine" belongs to the "new heaven and new earth" of apocalyptic thought, that is, to the transcendent order beyond space and time.

We turn now to predictions which make no direct mention of the Kingdom of God.

In the first place, Jesus is recorded to have predicted sufferings in store for Himself and His followers. It is often plausibly held that the forebodings of His own death which are repeatedly attributed to Jesus in the Gospels are of the nature of *vaticinia ex eventu*. The Church could not believe that their Lord had been ignorant of what lay before Him. It may freely be conceded that the precision of some of these predictions may be due to the Church's subsequent knowledge of the facts, but this admission does not necessarily carry with it the view that all forecasts of coming suffering are unhistorical.

We may observe (1) that the whole prophetic and apocalyp-

[26] The reading "when I drink it *with you*" is peculiar to Matthew, and is clearly a secondary addition to the original saying. Any interpretation therefore which finds the clue in the words "with you" is not based upon the earliest and best tradition. In Luke we have the form "until the Kingdom of God comes." For this evangelist therefore the saying contained a forecast of a second "coming" of the Kingdom of God; but the Lucan version here seems to be secondary. The corresponding saying which seems to come independently from Luke's special source runs (xxii. 15-16): "I earnestly desired to eat this passover with you before my passion [but I shall not do so], for I tell you, I shall never again eat it until it be fulfilled in the Kingdom of God." Here the Feast of the blessed (the Life of the Age to Come) is thought of as the "fulfilment" or complete realization of the symbolic rite of Passover.

tic tradition, which Jesus certainly recognized, anticipated tribulation for the people of God before the final triumph of the good cause; (2) that the history of many centuries had deeply implanted the idea that the prophet is called to suffering as a part of his mission; (3) that the death of John the Baptist had shown that this fate was still part of the prophetic calling; and (4) that it needed, not supernatural prescience, but the ordinary insight of an intelligent person, to see whither things were tending, at least during the later stages of the ministry.

When now we turn to the Gospel records we find that in all four of the main sources, or strands of tradition, which criticism recognizes, there are forecasts of persecution for the followers of Jesus, both direct and indirect. Such forecasts are indeed so emphatic and so characteristic of the whole temper and tone of the teaching that it seems impossible to attribute them all to the later reflections of the persecuted Church. The various contexts in which they occur leave it possible to doubt whether the sufferings anticipated were expected to come almost immediately, or at a later date. For example, one group of such predictions occurs in Matthew in the Charge given to the Twelve when they were sent out to preach and heal (x. 17-22), and in Mark in the final discourse (xiii. 9-13), just before the death of Jesus. In the latter case they are clearly taken to refer to the persecution of the Church as recorded in the Acts of the Apostles and elsewhere. In the former case the impression is that persecution might break out at any moment, perhaps even while the Twelve were out on their mission. In Luke some of the same group of predictions occur in a third different context (xii. 11-12).

It is clear that the occasion of such sayings was not clearly indicated in the earliest tradition. But it is noteworthy that a call to endure sufferings is in several passages of Mark and Luke associated with the theme of a journey to Jerusalem[27]; and indeed the impression which we gather from the Gospels as a whole is that Jesus led His followers up to the city with the express understanding that a crisis awaited them there which would involve acute suffering both for them and for Him. The most striking of such passages is Mk.

[27] Mk. x. 31-45, Lk. ix. 51-62, xiii. 22-24, xiv. 25-33.

x. 35-40. Here the sons of Zebedee are assured that they shall drink of the cup of which their Master drinks, and be baptized with His baptism. The purport of the words is not doubtful. The disciples are to share the fate of their Master, and surely to share His fate in the crisis which lies immediately before them.[28] In point of fact the followers of Jesus did not at that crisis share His fate. Strangely enough, the Jewish authorities seem to have been content with the death of the Leader, and to have left His followers alone. Naturally the Church sought fulfilment of this and other similar predictions in events which happened many years later.

In a passage which occurs in slightly differing forms in Mark and in the common material of Matthew and Luke, and therefore possesses the combined attestation of our two best sources, Jesus speaks of the coming sufferings of His disciples in the form of a call to "bear the cross"[29] (Mk. viii. 34, reproduced in Mt. xvi. 24, Lk. ix. 23; Mt. x. 38 = Lk. xiv. 27). As the cross was an only too familiar method of execution under Roman government, the suggestion is that He wished to prepare them not only for suffering but for death. There is a hint in the same direction in the "Q" saying, "Fear not them that kill the body" (Mt. x. 28 = Lk. xii. 4).

In this context of thought it becomes entirely credible that Jesus did, as the Gospels say, predict His own death. To what point in the ministry such predictions belong, is a question which for our purpose we need not answer. It is at any rate clear that at the Last Supper Jesus anticipated immediate death for Himself; but at this point it is equally clear that He expected His followers to survive. He passes

---

[28] It is customary at the present time to treat the prediction of "cup" and "baptism" for James and John as a *vaticinium ex eventu*, and even to use it to support the otherwise shaky evidence for an early martyrdom of John as well as James. This seems to me a singular way of treating evidence. On the face of it the prediction that the brothers should share the fate of their Master is one which was not, in its natural sense, fulfilled. That it should nevertheless have been preserved, is all in favour of the tradition.

[29] Dr. Torrey's attempt (*The Four Gospels: a New Translation*, p. 263) to show that σταυρός here represents the Aramaic z'qiph, and that this is to be taken in the sense of "yoke" (cf. ὁ ζυγός μου in Mt. xi. 29-30), is unconvincing, because he admits that he cannot cite any actual example of z'qiph = yoke.

the cup by, because He has done with this world; He gives it to His disciples because they must endure " the fellowship of His sufferings " in this world.

The most natural reconstruction of the facts from the evidence would seem to be that Jesus anticipated tribulation for Himself and His followers; that towards the close of His ministry He led His followers to Jerusalem with the expectation that He, and some at least of them, would suffer death at the hands of the authorities; and that at the last He went open-eyed to death Himself, predicting further tribulations for His followers after His death.

There is another group of predictions which refer to coming disasters for the Jewish people, their city and temple. According to Mk. xiv. 58, it was alleged against Jesus at His trial that He had said " I will destroy this temple made with hands, and in three days I will build another not made with hands." The same saying occurs in John ii. 19, in the form " Destroy this temple, and in three days I will raise it up ". Now it seems clear that the belief that Jesus had said something of this kind was an embarrassment to the early Church. Mark is concerned to invalidate the evidence given at the trial: it was never proved, he says, that Jesus had said this; there was a conflict of evidence (Mk. xiv. 59). John is concerned to show that the saying did not bear the meaning put upon it (ii. 21-22). But if Jesus did not say something of the kind, is it likely that the Church would have produced so embarrassing a saying? Mark himself avers (xiii. 2) that what Jesus had actually said was, " Do you see these great buildings? Not one stone will be left upon another without being pulled down."

And here attention must be called to a significant point which has not been sufficiently noticed. It is a practice of Mark, when he records something which seems to call for explanation, to introduce a private interview between Jesus and His disciples at which the matter is elucidated.[30] After the saying about the destruction of the temple he introduces such a private interview between Jesus and four disciples, at which the long " apocalyptic discourse " is delivered. That whole discourse is introduced primarily in order to set the saying about the destruction of the temple in its proper light.

[30] See Mk. iv. 10 sqq., vii. 17 sqq., ix. 11-13, 28-29, v. 10-12.

So far from having threatened to destroy the temple (Mark means) Jesus had predicted that after a long period of tribulation there would be a horrible act of sacrilege in the temple,[31] and then would follow a great tribulation in Judæa, and afterwards the final catastrophe, in which the whole universe would collapse. In this scheme the destruction of the temple is not explicitly mentioned, but it is implied that it would come as a sequel to the great sacrilege. It is not an impending historical event, still less an act which Jesus Himself had plotted, as His enemies alleged. Our evangelist would surely not have made so much pother about it if there had not been a good tradition (to be explained, or explained away) that Jesus had affronted the feelings of His Jewish hearers by predicting the ruin of their holy place.

In the " Q " material there is no such explicit prediction. But in Mt. xxiii. 37-38 = Lk. xiii. 34-35 we have an address to Jerusalem culminating in the declaration: " Your house is abandoned." The " house " may be the city of Jerusalem itself; more likely it is the temple, " Our holy and our beautiful house where our fathers praised thee " Is. lxiv. 11). It is abandoned, not, probably, by the worshippers, but by the divine presence which alone gives its significance.[32] The temple is not now, as God meant it to be, " a house of prayers for all nations "; it has become as it had become in the days of Jeremiah, " a brigand's hold " (Mk. xi. 17). As Jeremiah had predicted its ensuing destruction, so, we are to understand, did Jesus. In spite of Mark's attempt to associate the prediction with an apocalyptic catastrophe, it is most natural to suppose that Jesus pronounced the doom of the temple as an impending event in history.[33]

[31] As we have seen, Mark's forecast of coming events says nothing of a hostile capture of Jerusalem, with the burning of the temple. It seems therefore that the apocalyptic discourse was composed before the events of A.D. 70, and that the prediction of the destruction of the temple cannot be taken as a *vaticinium ex eventu*.

[32] We may compare the story in Josephus (*Bell Jud.*, VI, v 3, § 299) that before the capture of Jerusalem a mysterious voice was heard in the temple saying " Let us go hence."

[33] Have we (as E. A. Abbott, *The Fourfold Gospel*, v. p. 208, J. R. Coates, *The Christ of Revolution*, pp. 92-95) an implicit reference to the temple in Mk. xi. 23? " I tell you truly, whoever says to this mountain, ' Be removed, and be hurled into the sea '; and has no

We cannot but connect this doom of the temple with the various words of judgment upon the Jewish people and its leaders. The existing generation of Israel, according to the " Q " prophecy in Mt. xxiii. 34-36 = Lk. xi. 49-51, will bear the accumulated penalty of all righteous blood shed " from the blood of Abel to the blood of Zacharias."[34] As for the form in which this judgment is conceived, our Gospels in their existing form leave us in some doubt. Lk. xix. 43-44 predicts a siege of Jerusalem, in some detail; cf. also xxi. 20,

---

doubt in his heart, but believes that what he says is happening, he shall have it." Taken as a general statement that faith can do anything, this saying has always been something of a difficulty. But suppose " this mountain " is " the mountain of the Lord's house ", which according to prophecy should " in the last days . . . be established in the top of the mountains and exalted above the hills " (Is. ii. 2 = Mic. iv. 1). The hope of Israel had been that the temple should, on " the Day of the Lord " (when the Kingdom of God should be revealed), stand upon its lofty hill as the religious centre of the whole world. Jesus says, on the contrary, that, now that the Kingdom of God has come, the temple has no further place; it will be sunk, hill and all, into the sea. The " faith " by which this comes about is the acknowledgment that the Kingdom of God is here. There is much to be said for this interpretation. It is noteworthy that in the corresponding saying in Lk. xvii. 6 (which appears to be from " Q ", cf. Mt. xvii. 20), it is a fig-tree that is to be cast into the sea. The fig-tree, we know, was a symbol of the people of God. Whether it is the temple, or the Jewish community, the meaning is much the same. And here we probably have a clue to the episode of the blasted fig-tree (Mk. xi. 12-14, 20) which introduces the Marcan saying about the mountain. The " fig-tree " is Israel, now doomed to perpetual sterility. A parable has been made into an incident; unless indeed an act of " prophetic symbolism " underlies the story (see Wheeler Robinson, *Prophetic Symbolism*, in *Old Testament Essays*, edited by D. C. Simson. Griffin, 1927).

[34] It is customary at the present time to regard this passage as a citation from some lost " Wisdom " book. On this, I would refer to my note in *Mysterium Christi* (English edition), p. 57. Hypothetical " lost apocrypha " have played too large a part in some recent criticism. First find your apocryphon! As for Josephus's " Zacharias the son of Baruch " (*Bell. Jud.*, IV. v. 4, §§ 334 sqq.), why drag him in, when the last book of the Hebrew Canon records the martyrdom of Zacharias, as the first book records the death of Abel? Matthew no doubt *may* have known about the son of Baruch, and confused him with the prophet, the son of Berechiah, and both with the Zechariah of II Chron. xxiv. 21. But in any case Barachias was not in " Q ". I see, in short, no adequate ground for rejecting this prophecy as a word of Jesus. If the " lost apocryphon " should turn up, it may still be that Jesus quoted from it, as He certainly quoted from the Old Testament, and possibly from the Testaments of the Twelve Patriarchs.

where the investment of the city by enemy forces takes the place which in Mk. xiii. 14 is occupied by a sacrilege in the temple.[85] The context in Mark is fantastic, but nevertheless the prediction of xiii. 14-20 suggest an historical catastrophe. The command to flee to the mountains in Mk. xiii. 14 seems to correspond to the " oracle " which according to Eusebius (*Hist. Eccl.* III. v. 3) led the Christians of Jerusalem to desert the city in A.D. 66. If so, it is not likely to be a *vaticinium ex eventu.* The injunction, " He who is on the housetop must not come down to take up anything from his house, and he who is in the field must not turn to take up his coat,"[36] would admirably suit a supposed situation in which the quick-marching Roman armies are threatening Jerusalem; and the prayer that it might not happen in winter is appropriate to war conditions. In a purely supernatural " apocalyptic " tribulation summer or winter would matter little!

We may further adduce a passage peculiar to Luke, which nevertheless seems to bear the marks of historical veracity— the reference to the massacre of Galilaeans and the fall of the Tower of Siloam in Lk. xiii. 1-5. In themselves these incidents were comparatively inconspicuous. They are made to foreshadow judgment on Israel in the form of the sword of Rome and the collapse of the towers of Jerusalem. This quite incidental and allusive reference to the Roman peril seems to me to be significant.

The evidence is not entirely satisfactory, but it does appear, when all allowance has been made for the probable colouring of our tradition by the experience of the Church, that just as the Old Testament prophets saw in the Assyrian or the Baby-

[85] It is commonly held that Luke has here modified his Marcan source in the light of events known to him. I formerly shared this view, but further study has convinced me that it has no sufficient ground. The description of the siege in Luke has no specific traits in common with the historical siege of Jerusalem under Titus, but recalls the siege by Nebuchadnezzar in 586 B.C. as described in Old Testament prophecy and narrative. See my article in *Journal of Roman Studies,* vol. xxxvii (1947), pp. 47-54.

[36] Luke (xvii. 31) gives this saying, not in the Marcan context, but in a different and highly " apocalyptic " setting. As most of the material hereabouts belongs to the " Q " stratum, it may be that the saying about the housetop was also in " Q ", especially as there are some minute points in its wording in which Matthew and Luke agree against Mark.

lonian peril the form in which divine judgment on Israel was
approaching, so Jesus saw in the growing menace of a clash
with Rome a token of coming disaster, in which the sins
of the Jewish people would meet their retribution. Our Gospels
were written at a time, and for a public, to which the political
fortunes of Judæa had little relevance.[37] It is not surprising
if the historical realism of some of the sayings of Jesus has been
slurred over in a generalized eschatological scheme. It appears
that the prophets made use of earlier mythological conceptions
of " The Day of Jehovah," and rationalized and moralized them
in terms of the historical situation in their day. Their predictions were in many cases re-absorbed (so to speak) into
mythology by the apocalyptists. It may well be that a similar
tendency has affected the Gospel records of the sayings of
Jesus.

We conclude that Jesus uttered predictions comparable with
those of the Old Testament prophets, that is to say, He forecast historical developments of the situation in which He
stood. In particular, He forecast a crisis in which He Himself
should die and His followers suffer severe persecution; and He
forecast historical disaster for the Jewish people and their
temple.

We may now ask whether there is any evidence to show
how the crisis which brings the death of Jesus is to be related to the disasters coming upon the Jewish people. Actually
the death of Jesus was separated from the fall of Jerusalem
by about forty years, and we must expect the knowledge of this
fact to have coloured our records. But we observe that it
is " this generation " upon which the retribution for the blood
of the righteous is to fall (Mt. xxiii. 35-36 = Lk. xi. 50-51).
Now Mark, in reporting the forecast of the coming disasters
makes Jesus say that the generation He addresses will experience not only these disasters, but also the final collapse of
the universe: " This generation will not pass away until *all*
these things have happened " (xiii. 30). No doubt when Mark
wrote, and even in A.D. 70, there were many people alive who

[37] For a persuasive exposition of the bearing of the teaching of
Jesus upon the Judæo-Roman situation, see Vladimir Simkhovitch,
Towards the Understanding of Jesus (Macmillan, 1923).

were also alive in A.D. 29.[38] But the generation which suffered the calamities of the Roman war was not, in any real sense, the same generation as that of forty years before. We must suppose that historical exigencies have led to a certain expansion of the interim period, and that Jesus actually expected the tribulation of Judæa to follow more closely upon His own death. We must add that the saying about the destruction of the temple, whatever its original form, must have been capable of being understood as an immediate menace, and not a forecast of something to happen in the comparatively remote future.

Consider again the following important passage, which occurs both in Matthew and in Luke. In Luke it is embedded in a context full of such parallels with Matthew, and therefore may fairly be attributed to a common source, written or oral, even though the wording differs considerably : —[39]

MT. x. 34-36	LK. XII. 49-53
"Do not suppose that I came to cast peace upon the earth. I came not to cast peace but a sword. For I came to set a man at variance with his father, a daughter with her mother, and a daughter-in-law with her mother-in-law; and a man's enemies will be the members of his household."	"I came to cast fire upon the earth, and how I wish it were already kindled![40] I have a baptism to undergo, and how I am cramped until it is accomplished! Do you think I came to give peace on earth? No, I tell you, but division! For from this time on there will be five in one house divided, three against

[38] But how many of them were more than children at the time? A study of sepulchral inscriptions of the Roman Empire leads to the conclusion which is probable on other grounds, that the average adult expectation of life was far shorter than it is to-day.

[39] To determine the original form of the saying would be a delicate task. Εἰρήνην βαλεῖν is an odd expression; πῦρ βαλεῖν ἐπί "to set fire to," is more natural, and probably more original. The parallelized form of the saying in Luke is further in favour of his version at this point, and the figure of "baptism" for sufferings is attested by Mk. x. 38-39. On the other hand διαμερισμός would seem to have been substituted for μάχαιραν to avoid an obvious possibility of misunderstanding.

[40] This translation presupposes that the Greek is a somewhat clumsy rendering of an Aramaic idiom. See Gressmann and Torrey, ad. loc. If this is right, it is a further point in favour of the Lucan version.

> two and two against three.
> They will be divided, father
> against son and son against
> father, mother against daugh-
> ter and daughter against
> mother, mother-in-law against
> daughter-in-law and daughter-
> in-law against mother-in-law."

A reference to various prophetic and apocalyptic passages[41] will show that this description of division among families is part of the traditional picture of " red ruin and the breaking-up of laws," and appropriate to the " eschatological " tribulation. Mark has rationalized the saying in a forecast of the treachery within families which Christians actually experience in times of persecution (xiii. 12). The fact that the saying was known to him, as well as to the compiler of " Q ", confirms its authenticity, but the " Q " version is to be preferred. According to this, Jesus expected that the crisis which His ministry was bringing about would issue in a general upheaval; and if the Lucan version is to be trusted, He connected this directly with His own " baptism " of suffering. In His forecast of history we recognise the characteristic " foreshortening " of prophetic vision.

It certainly looks as if Jesus conceived His ministry as moving rapidly to a crisis, which would bring about His own death, the acute persecution of His disciples, and a general upheaval in which the power of Rome would make an end of the Jewish nation, its city and temple. If he did speak in such terms, it is not surprising that, when things did not turn out precisely so, His sayings should have been to some extent remoulded to fit the course of events.

It is, however, important to make it clear that this foresight is not of the nature of mere clairvoyance. It is in the first place insight into the actual situation. The perception that the religion of the temple has no absolute significance dramatizes itself in a picture of its actual destruction. The perception that the historic Jewish community as at

[41] See Micah vii. 6; Is. xix. 2; Ezek. xxxviii. 21; Jubilees xxiii. 16, 19; II Baruch lxx. 3-7; II Esdras vi. 24.

present constituted is not serving the advancing purpose of God, dramatizes itself in the vision of its end amid the horrors of war and social upheaval. Whether or not the predictions were to be fulfilled in the actual course of history, the essential spiritual judgment upon the situation stands. As a matter of fact, Jerusalem did fall, the temple was destroyed, and the Jewish community as a political institution came to an end. These things did not happen exactly in the way Jesus predicted, but at least they provided an impressive corroboration in history of His discernment of inevitable tendencies, arising out of a spiritual estimate of the situation.

This principle, that foresight is primarily insight, and that predictions, however concrete and true to the historical situation, are primarily a dramatization of spiritual judgments, is equally applicable to the classical prophets of the O.T. In them also we observe the shortening of historical perspective. When the profound realities underlying a situation are depicted in the dramatic form of historical prediction, the certainty and inevitability of the spiritual processes involved are expressed in terms of the immediate imminence of the event. The proposition, " A is involved in B " (by the logic of the moral and spiritual order), becomes " A will follow immediately upon B." The actual time-process is not so simple or direct. But the time-scale is irrelevant to the ultimate significance of history. " One day is with the Lord as a thousand years, and a thousand years as one day "—and not with the Lord only, but with the philosophical historian.[42] It is enough if we can see that the great tendencies of history correspond with the spiritual principles enunciated by the prophets, whether at short range or at long. In so far as they do, *die Weltgeschichte ist das Weltgericht.*

The predictions which we have considered may be compared with the prophetic forecasts of disaster in the O.T.—the " eschatology of woe," as it is sometimes called (" *Unheils-*

[42] The lapse of time before civilization began is measured in millenia, the life of civilizations in centuries; and civilizations differ in the relative length of the periods during which they grew, flourished and declined. But these differences are not of primary importance if we are considering the causes, nature and value of civilization.

eschatologie "). In most of the O.T. prophets the eschatology of woe is balanced by an "eschatology of bliss" (" *Heils-eschatologie "*). After the disaster Jehovah will have mercy on His people and give them marvellous prosperity. In the early prophets this epoch of prosperity is conceived in historical though miraculous terms—victory over enemies, miraculous fruitfulness of the land, and the like. In the apocalypses these temporal blessings are either supplemented or replaced by the wholly supernatural bliss of " The Age to Come."

Now it is extremely difficult to find in the sayings of Jesus anything which could point to an " eschatology of bliss " on the historical or temporal plane, corresponding to the " eschatology of woe " which we have considered.

There are in fact only two passages in the Gospels which could with any show of reason be held to bear such a meaning. According to Mark (and John) the prediction of the fall of the temple was accompanied with the assurance " In three days I will build another temple " (or, " I will raise it up ") And there is a " Q " saying, whose exact original form it is difficult to reconstruct out of the varying versions in Mt. xix. 28, Lk. xxii. 28-30, but which in any case spoke of the Twelve as " judging the twelve tribes of Israel." These two sayings taken by themselves, might conceivably be understood to mean that after predicting the ruin of the temple and of the Jewish state, Jesus went on, after the manner of the prophets, to predict that the Jewish state would be restored, with Himself as King and His disciples as His ministers of state, and that He would miraculously rebuild the temple. It is true that Mark and Matthew, in the respective contexts, have been at pains to guard against such an interpretation. Mark throws doubt upon the authenticity of the saying about the temple, and in any case he gives it in a form which contrasts the temple " made with hands," which is to be destroyed, with a temple " not made with hands " which is to take its place. But the epithets are not present in the Johannine form of the saying, and they recall the vocabulary of the Acts and the Epistles.[48]

---

[43] Χειροποίητος as an epithet of the temple, Ac. vii. 47, xvii. 24; Heb. ix. 11, 24; cf. also Eph. ii. 11: ἀχειροποίητος, II Cor. v. 1; Col. ii. 11. The epithets do not occur in Matthew or Luke.

Nor, in spite of Mark's aspersions upon the witnesses, is there good reason to deny the substantial authenticity of the saying. As for the judging of the tribes, Matthew has made it clear that it is to take place " at the rebirth," i.e. in the transcendent order beyond history. This however may be discounted on the score of this evangelist's known tendency to emphasize the apocalyptic element. In the Lucan form the prediction might quite well be historical in character.

The question is whether we are justified, on the ground of the *prima facie* meaning of these two sayings, in reversing the general impression created by the sayings of Jesus as a whole, by the Gospel narrative, and by the procedure of the Church after its Founder's death, the impression, namely, that He dissociated Himself from national aspirations. Attempts have indeed been made in various quarters to show that the intention of Jesus was to bring about a political or social revolution, and that after the failure the Church sedulously covered its tracks.[44] Such attempts, when worked out in detail, serve only to show how arbitrarily it is necessary to deal with the evidence, and how much has to be supplied by sheer speculation, to give any such results. But unless a drastic reconstruction of the whole story could be effected, we are obliged to suppose that the two sayings in question are susceptible of some other meaning than that of an historical forecast.

The saying about the judging of the tribes is probably to be placed, where Matthew places it, in the context of ideas about Doomsday and the Day of the Son of Man, which I shall presently consider. The building of the temple " not made with hands " is similarly to be associated with the apocalyptic idea of " the restoration of all things."

We conclude that on the historical plane there is no " eschatology of bliss " in the sayings of Jesus. He gave no promise that the future would bring with it any such perfection of human society as some Jewish thinkers had predicted under the form of a restored kingdom of David. He declared that the Kingdom of God had come. When He spoke of it in terms of the future, His words suggest, not

[44] Notably by R. Eisler, *The Messiah Jesus and John the Baptist* (English trans., 1931).

any readjustment of conditions on this earth, but the glories of a world beyond this.

How then are we to relate the "historical" predictions of suffering and death, and of disasters upon the Jewish people, to the declaration that the Kingdom of God has come?

In view of this declaration it is not permissible, for example, to represent the death of Jesus as in any sense the condition precedent to the coming of the Kingdom of God. We may not say that He died "to bring in the Kingdom"; that His death was the "price" of its coming; or that He died to bring about the repentance without which it could not come. These and similar statements, in one form or another, are often found in modern attempts to explain the matter. But they are all confuted by the fact that Jesus before His death declared that the Kingdom of God had come.[45]

The point may be illustrated by comparing a passage in a contemporary apocalypse. *The Assumption of Moses* was composed, according to Charles's dating,[46] during the lifetime of Jesus. It contains one of the very rare direct allusions to the Kingdom of God in apocalyptic literature. In chap. ix. we have a prophecy about one Taxo and his sons, who in the days when the servants of God are persecuted, will deliberately give themselves over to a martyr death; " *and then,*" we read in chap. x, "and then His Kingdom shall appear throughout all His creation." The death of the martyrs is the condition precedent to the appearance of the Kingdom of God. The situation in the Gospels is different. Jesus proclaims

---

[45] I will not discuss the view that Jesus at first declared that the Kingdom of God had come, and afterwards withdrew the statement as too optimistic. It would need some very clear evidence to make it credible that Jesus was ever the prey of such easy optimism, which is moreover alien to the whole prophetic tradition. If He declared that the Kingdom of God had come, it must surely have been in the teeth of the facts which seemed to contradict Him. No doubt, if we understood Him to say that the Kingdom of God would come very soon, it would be easier to suppose that He afterwards lengthened the interval; but this is not what He said, though much modern criticism slips out of the difficulty by reading ἔφθασεν as if it were μόνον οὐκ ἔφθασεν, a perfectly good idiom which might have been used if this had been the meaning intended.

[46] *The Assumption of Moses*, 1897, pp. lv-lviii. Charles arrives at the date A.D. 7-30.

that the Kingdom of God has come, and He also foretells suffering and death for Himself and disasters upon Israel. In some
sense therefore this "eschatology of woe" falls within the
Kingdom of God.

Let us then go back to the common underlying meaning
of the expression "The Kingdom of God" in all its various
uses. It means God exercising His kingly rule among men.
In particular it implies that the divine power is effectively
at issue with the evil in the world, making an end of "the
kingdom of the enemy." In this sense judgment is a function
of the Kingdom of God. When it comes in history, it brings
the effective condemnation of sin. We can understand that
Jesus saw in the crisis which His ministry was bringing to
a head, an effective judgment on the sin of Israel. The purpose
of God, indeed, in asserting His sovereignty in the world is
to confer on men "eternal life," and to "receive His kingdom" is to "enter into life." But to reject God is to pronounce
judgment upon oneself. "He who rejects me, rejects Him
that sent me," said Jesus (Lk. x. 16).

In rejecting Him, the Jewish nation rejected the Kingdom
of God. They thereby shut themselves out from the bliss
of the Kingdom, but brought themselves under the judgment of
the Kingdom. In weal or woe, the Kingdom of God came
upon them.

Can we then bring the death of Jesus under this same
category? I will venture to turn for an answer to the epistles
of Paul. This will no doubt seem to some readers an illegitimate dragging-in of theology. But Paul was not only the
first Christian theologian. He is also our earliest authority
for the facts and beliefs upon which the Christian religion rests.
He came in contact with the Christian tradition, through its
original bearers, during the first decade after the Crucifixion.
After that he had for many years little contact with the Aramaic-
speaking wing of the Church,[47] in which the Synoptic

[47] See Gal. i. 18-24. The conversion of Paul cannot well be dated
later than about A.D. 34. Before that he had been in (hostile) contact
with the Hellenistic Christians led by Stephen. Three years later he
spent a fortnight in Jerusalem as the guest of Peter. After that he
remained for fourteen years "unknown by face" to the Christians of
Judæa. He did not receive his gospel from any man, he says; but it is
unlikely that he remained ignorant either of the facts which were

tradition grew up. We may regard the Pauline type of Christian thought as a development from the original tradition. parallel to the development which produced the Synoptic Gospels.[48] While we must always allow fully for Paul's originality, we cannot brush aside his contribution to an understanding of the early tradition, especially as we have no evidence that his differences with Peter extended beyond the field of missionary policy to the fundamentals of the Christian tradition itself.

Now Paul says that through the death of Jesus God triumphed over principalities and powers (Col. ii. 15). We have seen that in apocalypse the final victory over " the kingdom of the enemy " is the coming of the Kingdom of God; and that in the Synoptic Gospels the exorcisms of Jesus are treated as signs of this victory and so of the coming of the Kingdom. Paul adds that His death also was a means of God's victory over the powers of evil. He says further that through the death of Jesus God manifested His righteousness (Rom. iii. 25), and condemned sin (Rom. viii. 3). But the manifestation of the righteousness of God, and judgment upon sin, are essential elements in the idea of the Kingdom of God. Paul therefore understood that the death of Jesus fell within the Kingdom of God, as a part of the effective assertion of God's sovereign rule in the world.

There was surely something in the original tradition upon which he could base such an interpretation, and in any case it does provide an explanation for the recorded fact that Jesus declared at once that the Kingdom of God had come, and that He Himself must die. If there is no parallel or anticipation of such an idea in the Jewish background of Christian thought, that is nothing against it. As we have seen, the declaration that the Kingdom of God has come breaks up, in any case, the old eschatological scheme, and makes room for a new set of ideas. Further, the teaching of Jesus upon the character of God and His attitude to men

---

common knowledge, or of the interpretation of these facts in the Petrine circle. Or what did he and Cephas talk about for a fortnight?

[48] Pauline influence upon the Synoptic Gospels is often alleged, but the evidence for it amounts to very little.

—His unqualified benevolence and beneficence towards all
His creatures, His unlimited forgiveness, His desire to seek
and to save the lost—leads necessarily to a new view of
what it means for God's righteousness to be manifested, and
for sin to be condemned. Our attempt to determine the
relation between the coming of the Kingdom of God and
the death of Jesus has led to the necessity for a theology
according to which God's opposition to evil is shown in
the suffering of its worst assaults, and the condemnation of sin
is its self-exhibition as " exceeding sinful " in the presence
of the revealed love of God. While formally the new and
original element in the teaching of Jesus is that the Kingdom
of God, long expected, has come, there is an even more profound originality in the new content given to the idea through
His revelation of God Himself.[49]

Thus the course of events which outwardly is a series of
disasters holds within it a revelation of the glory of God,
for those who have insight. This is the " mystery of the
Kingdom of God "; not only that the *eschaton*, that which
belongs properly to the realm of the " wholly other," is now
matter of actual experience, but that it is experienced in the
paradoxical form of the suffering and death of God's representative. Behind or within the paradoxical turn of events lies
that timeless reality which is the kingdom, the power and
the glory of the blessed God.

[49] On this see Otto, *op. cit.*, p. 83. "All His works and words . . .
are directly or indirectly inspired by the idea of a divine power breaking
in, to *save*. This has its immediate correlate in the ' new ' God whom
He brings, the God who does not consume sinners, but *seeks*
sinners; the Father-God, who has now once again *drawn near*
out of His transcendence, who asked for the child-mind and child-like
trust " (my translation, his italics).

Chapter III

THE DAY OF THE SON OF MAN

So far we have considered predictions which appear to refer to coming events within the historical order. We must now turn to other predictions to which it is difficult to give such a reference.

First we must notice a group of sayings in " Q " which make use of the traditional eschatological conception of Dooms-day (variously called " the Judgment," " the Day of Judgment," or " that Day "). In Mt. xi. 21-22 = Lk. x. 13-14 we read, " Woe to you, Chorazin! Woe to you, Bethsaida! For if the works of power which happened in you had happened in Tyre and Sidon, they would long ago have repented in sackcloth and ashes." (So far the saying means no more than that the Phœnician cities, whose territory, contiguous with Galilee, Jesus visited, would have been a more responsive public for his work than His own cities; but the saying proceeds) " It will be more tolerable for Tyre and Sidon on the [day of] judgment than for you."

Again in Mt. x. 15 = Lk. x. 12, any city which does not respond to the appeal of the Twelve is condemned in the words, " It will be more tolerable for Sodom [and Gomorrah] on the day of judgment [or ' on that Day '] than for you." What is the implication of such sayings? The judgment of Judæa, as we have seen, seems to be expressed in terms of the horrors of war and social upheaval; but it is impossible to suppose that Tyre and Sidon are promised an easier lot in that impending historical tribulation. They had nothing to fear from Rome. And as for Sodom and Gomorrah, *their* judgment, in an historical sense, had taken place ages ago.

Again, in Mt. xii. 41-47 = Lk. xi. 31-32, the men of Nineveh, contemporaries of the prophet Jonah, and the Queen of the South, a contemporary of Solomon, are to appear "in the judgment " as witnesses against the Jews who heard and ignored the preaching of Jesus.

If in such passages the idea of the Day of Judgment is to be taken literally and realistically, we are obliged to think of a Great Assize in which individuals long dead, and peoples long extinct, play their part. It is therefore outside the historical order. The intention at any rate of the sayings is clear. The Rabbis counted the men of Sodom among those who had notably " no part in the Life of the Age to Come."[1] Jesus therefore says in effect to His hearers, " Even those whom you consider the most hopeless of sinners are less hopeless than those who refuse to hear the Gospel." Similarly in His reference to Tyre and Sidon He is echoing the prophetic words, " You only have I known of all the families of the earth, therefore upon you I will visit all your iniquities. . . . Are ye not as the children of the Ethiopians unto me, O children of Israel?" (Amos iii. 2, ix. 7); and the references to Nineveh and the Queen of Sheba are in the same spirit. There is no independent interest in the Day of Judgment as such, or in the fate of Gentiles in the judgment. The time-honoured image of a Last Judgment is simply assumed, and used to give vividness and force to solemn warnings.

There is another group of sayings in " Q " which speak of the Day of the Son of Man.[2] According to Mt. xxiv. 37-39 =Lk. xvii. 26-27, that Day will be like Noah's Deluge, coming suddenly and unexpectedly upon people thoughtlessly engaged in the ordinary occupations of life. According to Mt. xxiv. 27 =Lk. xvii. 24, it will be like a flash of lightning spanning the whole vault of heaven at once. According to Mk. xiii. 24-26, the sun and moon will cease to shine, the stars will fall from

---

[1] See tractate *Sanhedrin*, 10, 3, quoted by Strack-Billerbeck on Mt. x. 15.

[2] The expression " the Day of the Son of Man," corresponding closely to the O.T. expression " The Day of Jehovah," is implied in Lk. xvii. 24, ουτως ἔσται ὁ υἱὸς τοῦ ἀνθρώπου ἐν τῇ ἡμέρᾳ αὐτοῦ, but the actual phrase does not appear in the Gospels. Luke has " the days of the Son of Man " (xvii. 26, and in a passage peculiar to him, xvii. 22). Matthew uses the stereotyped phrase, ἡ παρουσία τοῦ υιοῦ τοῦ ἀνθρώπου, in various contexts. As the word παρουσία is peculiar to him, we may reasonably doubt whether it occurred in the earliest tradition. It seems most likely that the original term underlying the variety is " The Day of the Son of Man."

heaven, and all the celestial " powers "[3] will be shaken, and *then* " they will see the Son of Man coming in the clouds with much power and glory." But here this cosmic catastrophe will be preceded by a long series of signs. It is not sudden and unexpected, like Noah's flood. After all the events forecast in Mk. xiii. 14-25 it is safe to assume that people will no longer be eating and drinking, marrying and being married! The two accounts are inconsistent, and of the two we must certainly prefer that of " Q ". Our two earliest sources however agree in representing the Day of the Son of Man as a super- natural event, of universal significance. " Q " emphasises its difference from any historical event. Of any event in history one can say that it happens here or there. Of the Day of the Son of Man one must not say " Lo, here! " or " Lo there! " because it is like a flash of lightning visible everywhere at once.[4]

[3] The δυνάμεις are the discarnate intelligences supposed to inhabit and control the astral universe, among the Jews identified with orders of angels. See my book, *The Bible and the Greeks*, pp. 16-19, 109-111.
[4] This is perhaps the place to consider a passage peculiar to Luke which has a certain similarity to the " Q " saying before us (Lk. xvii. 20-21); " The Kingdom of God does not come with observation " (i.e. it is not something you can watch for, as astronomers watch for the conjunctions of the heavenly bodies), " nor will they say, ' Lo here, or there!' For behold the Kingdom of God is ἐντὸς ὑμῶν—among you "? or " within you "? The former translation is nowadays almost uni- versally preferred. But (i) ἐντὸς is properly a strengthened form of ἐν used where it is important to exclude any of the possible meanings of that preposition other than " inside." The only approximations to the meaning " among " which are cited (Xenophon, *Anabasis*, I, 10, 3, *Hellenica*, II, 8, 19) are not, I think, clear exceptions to the rule. (ii) When Luke means " among ", he says ἐν μέσῳ, an expression which occurrs about a dozen times in the Third Gospel and the Acts. If he meant " among " here, why did he vary his usage? (iii) If appeal be made to an underlying Aramaic, the prepositions in that language meaning respectively " among " and " within " are distinct, and there is no reason why a competent translator should confuse them. (iv) " Among " does not give logical sense. A thing which is " among you " is localized in space, more or less. On the other hand you cannot say " Lo here, or there! " of that which is " within," and the Kingdom of God is said not to be localized in space, *because* it is ἐντὸς ὑμῶν. This might be understood as the counterpart of the " Q " saying dis- cussed above: the Day of the Son of Man is not localized in space (or time) because it is instantaneous and ubiquitous; the Kingdom of God is not localized because it is " within you." In other words, the ulti- mate reality, though it is revealed in history, essentially belongs to the

The purpose or consequence of the coming of the Son of Man is not clearly stated in our earliest sources. The First Gospel gives a short apocalypse (often miscalled the Parable of the Sheep and Goats[5]), in which the traditional scene of the Last Judgment is depicted in vivid colours, with the Son of Man as judge. There is however no direct confirmation of this in our other sources.[6] In Mk. xiii. 27, the Son of Man when He comes, " will send his angels and gather the elect from the four winds, from edge of heaven to edge of earth." In " Q " it appears from a comparison of Mt. xxiv. 37-40 with Lk. xvii. 23-35 that the saying about Noah's flood was followed, either immediately or at no long interval, by a double saying in parallelism, of which the second member is identical in the two Gospels, while the first has different forms:

MATTHEW	LUKE
" Then there will be two	" On that night there will

---

spiritual order, where the categories of space and time are not applicable. There is however another possible meaning. In the *Harvard Theological Review*, vol. xli, no. 1 (1948), C. H. Roberts argued persuasively, on the basis of evidence from papyri and elsewhere, that ἐντὸς ὑμῶν means " in your hands," " within your power." That is, the Kingdom of God is not something for which you have to watch anxiously (οὐ μετὰ παρατηρήσεως), but is an available possibility here and now, for those who are willing to " receive it as a little child." There is, I think, more to be said for the substantial authenticity of the Lucan saying than is generally admitted. But as it is not one of the passages clearly belonging to the oldest tradition, I am not using it in this discussion.

[5] Mt. xxv. 31-46. It does not conform to the parabolic type, but belongs to the same class as the judgment scenes in Enoch and other apocalypses. The only parabolic element in it is the simile of the shepherd separating the sheep and the goats, and this is a passing allusion; sheep and goats play no part in the main scene. The climax of the passage is to be found in the two sayings, xxv. 40, 45, which are parallel to Mt. x. 40-42, Mk. ix. 37. The judgment scene was probably composed to give a vivid, dramatic setting to these sayings.

[6] The same idea recurs in Mt. xvi. 27, but as we shall see, this is a Matthæan rewriting of a passage in Mark, which itself is probably less original than a corresponding saying in " Q." In the more original forms of the saying the Son of Man (or Jesus) appears not as judge, but as advocate. See Bacon, *The Other Comforter*, in *Expositor*, Oct., 1917, p. 280.

men in the field; one is taken and one is left.

" There will be two women grinding at the mill; one is taken and one is left."

be two men in one bed; the one will be taken and the other will be left.

" There will be two women grinding together; the one will be taken and the other will be left."[7]

The purport of these words is difficult to determine. It is not even clear whether the one taken or the one left has the better lot. The saying has in common with the saying which precedes it the idea of a sudden event overtaking people engaged in the ordinary occupations of life. This sudden event, it is suggested, will make a sharp distinction between the fate of individuals who up to that moment were in close association. If the connection of the two sayings is original, this event will be the Day of the Son of Man, bringing a selective judgment on individuals; but in this case the judgment is not conceived as a Great Assize in a world beyond this, in which communities like Sodom and Tyre, Bethsaida and Chorazin, appear before the Judgment-seat. It is something which supervenes directly upon the everyday life of individuals. If however the two sayings had originally no connection (as is very possible, for even " Q " is admittedly a compilation of originally independent sayings), we should naturally take the saying " one taken and the other left " as a true parable, and the question of its application would be an open one.[8]

[7] Inferior MSS. of Luke add here the two men in a field; but this is no part of the original text of this Gospel. The Synoptic situation is as follows: Matthew gives the saying " one taken and the other left " directly after the saying about Noah's Flood. Luke interposes (a) a second example of sudden disaster, that of Sodom; (b) the saying " do not come down from the housetop "; (c) the warning example of Lot's wife; (d) the saying " He who seeks to save his soul shall lose it . . ." Of these (d) is a floating saying, which crops up in several various contexts in all Gospels; (b) is given by Mark in the apocalyptic discourse, and as we have seen is best connected with the forecast of war.

[8] A. T. Cadoux, op. cit. pp. 195-196, suggests that the parable gives a picture of " the press-gang at work." That may well be so. But the " moral " he draws, " opportunity seeks the man and makes its selection," seems too flat and general. May the reference have been to the selective effect of the call of Jesus? James and John were in the boat

Even more clearly parabolic is the other saying which Luke gives immediately after this one, and Matthew appends to the saying about the lightning flash: "Wherever the carcase is, there the vultures will gather."[9] The idea surely is that there are certain conjunctions of phenomena which are quite constant and inevitable, so that if the one is observed, the other may be inferred; but what phenomena are in view we cannot say.

We are thus left with only vague indications of the rôle which the Son of Man is expected to play "in His Day." It is not made clear that the Day of the Son of Man is identical with the Day of Judgment, though it is natural to suppose that it is; but that the Son of Man Himself is judge is not stated in our earliest sources, nor is the form which the judgment will take made plain.

The matter is complicated by the fact that Jesus is represented in the Gospels as using the title "The Son of Man" with reference to Himself. Whether in this they are true to historical fact is a question about which there is a still unsettled controversy. It is certainly true that our Gospels show a tendency to insert the phrase "The Son of Man" into contexts where criticism shows that the original tradition made Jesus say "I," and it is argued that wherever the expression is used with reference to Jesus Himself it is secondary. Further, it cannot be denied that in unquestionably genuine passages (such as those we have just noticed) Jesus is made to refer to "The Son of Man" without the least suggestion that He is speaking of Himself.

On the other hand we must observe that in *all* our primary Gospel sources Jesus is identified with the Son of Man. That identification therefore at least belongs to an extremely early stage of the tradition. Moreover, the theory I have mentioned assumes that "The Son of Man" was at some stage a current

---

with Zebedee their father; the sons were taken, the father left with the hired servants (Mk. i. 19-20).

[9] Mt. xxiv. 28, Lk. xvii. 37. It has been suggested that the ἀετοί are Roman eagles, and that this is a forecast of the war. But though some eagles will eat carrion, the vulture is the bird which characteristically watches for the slain. 'Αετός is here probably the vulture, as in some places in the LXX.

Messianic designation for Jesus, and as such was interpolated into the records of His life and teaching. But we have no independent evidence of any such stage. There is only one passage in the N.T. outside the Gospels in which the expression is so used. In the Gospels themselves it is never used except in the mouth of Jesus.[10] In contrast, we know that the titles " The Messiah " and " The Lord " were current in the Church; yet in the Gospels Jesus is only exceptionally representetd as applying either to Himself.[11] The terms most familiar in the Church are recognized as inappropriate in the mouth of Jesus; the term " The Son of Man," which is seldom used in referring to Jesus, is represented as His most characteristic self-designation. This can best be accounted for if He did in fact so describe Himself. If that was so, we can well understand that the growing tradition tended to introduce the term " The Son of Man " into sayings which did not originally contain it. If not, it is difficult to understand why it should have appeared so frequently in sayings of Jesus, without penetrating

[10] Ac. vii. 56. Jn. xii. 34 is no real exception.

[11] Χριστός is not found in the " Q " passages. In Mark it occurs only twice in the mouth of Jesus, (a) ix. 41, where a comparison with Mt. x. 42 will suggest a doubt whether the words ὅτι χριστοῦ ἐστε stood in the earlier tradition; (b) xii. 35, where Jesus speaks of " the Messiah " as a personage in Jewish theology, without suggesting that He is Himself that personage. In passages peculiar to Matthew it is found once only in the mouth of Jesus, xxiii. 10, and a comparison with xxiii. 8 will suggest that these two sayings are doublets, and that xxiii, 8, which does not contain the word χριστός, is the earlier form. In Lk. xxiv. 46 it occurs in a brief summary of the teaching of Jesus after the Resurrection; it is not elsewhere found in this Gospel in the mouth of Jesus. On the other hand, it is comparatively frequent in the mouths of other persons and in passages where the evangelists speak in their own person, accurately reflecting the usage in the Church. Κύριος is put into the mouth of Jesus, with reference to Himself, twice in Mark, (a) ii. 28 (" Lord of the Sabbath "), (b) xi. 3 (in v. 19, xii. 11, 29-30, 36, xiii. 20, Κύριος is Jehovah, and in xii. 36-37 the " Messiah " is a theological figure); in " Q " there is only the passage, Mt. vii. 21, Lk. vi. 46, where Jesus rebukes those who address Him, Κύριε, Κύριε. Of examples of such address we have in Mark only vii. 28 (and a variant reading in x. 51), and here it seems no more than the customary courtesy title, " Sir." In Matthew and Luke the number of such cases is considerably increased, and the latter uses κύριος also in narrative, but neither of them makes Jesus speak of Himself as such, if we except parabolic contexts. In face of all this, can we assume that the Church would feel itself free to put into the mouth of Jesus a title which He did not actually use?

into the narrative. To apply the term " The Son of Man," with its " apocalyptic " and " eschatological " associations, to a living man, is no doubt a paradox; but it is also a paradox to say that the Kingdom of God, itself an " eschatological " fact, has come in history.

Assuming, then, that Jesus did speak of Himself as " The Son of Man," we have to think of Him as in some sense the central figure in the " Day of the Son of Man " predicted in the passages we have already considered. To these we must add Mk. xiv. 62. Here Jesus, questioned by the High Priest, " Are you the Messiah, the Son of the Blessed?" replies, " I am; and you will see ' The Son of Man seated on the right hand of the Power and coming with the clouds of heaven."[12] The words are a somewhat free citation of Dan. vii. 13, with a glance at Ps. cx. 1. The passage in Daniel describes an apocalyptic vision, in which mythological figures in the forms of beasts are overcome by " one like a son of man," i.e. by a figure of human form. The vision is then interpreted. The " beasts " stand for pagan empires; the Son of Man stands for " the people of the saints Most High."[13] The vision means

[12] For those critics who regard the examination before the High Priest as a fictitious scene devised to provide a setting for an explicit confession of Messiahship on the part of Jesus (the only such confession in the earlier tradition), it is of course out of the question to treat this citation as an historical utterance. But it is in accordance with legal procedure attested for other provinces that the local authority should perform the function of *juge d'instruction*, and prepare the charge to be preferred before the higher court. That the charge preferred before the Procurator was that of claiming to be "King of the Jews" seems beyond reasonable doubt. The claim to Messiahship must therefore have been investigated by the Sanhedrin; and as the case was undefended in the Procurator's court, we may take it that Jesus admitted His claim. But it would be in accordance with the general implications of the Gospel record if He brushed aside the title "Messiah" and substituted "the Son of Man." It is no doubt possible that the precise formulation of His answer in terms of the prophecy of Daniel is due to the early Church. If so, we have no evidence regarding the way in which Jesus connected His ministry as "Son of Man" with the coming "Day of the Son of Man." But we may be content, provisionally, to accept the evidence of our earliest source.

[13] It is especially noteworthy that the interpretation of the vision of the Son of Man (Dan. vii. 13-14) is given in vii. 22 in the words, ἔφθασεν ὁ καιρός, καὶ τὴν βασιλείαν κατέσχον οἱ ἅγιοι, which as we have seen (p. 28) seem to be echoed in the words of Jesus, ἔφθασεν ἐφ᾽ ὑμᾶς ἡ βασιλεία τοῦ θεοῦ.

that the Jewish people will at the end step into the place of the pagan world-empires, and so the Kingdom of God will be realized on earth. The vision is symbolical. The historical reality corresponding to it is the expected emergence of an independent and sovereign Jewish state. The "Son of Man" has as much or as little reality as the "beasts" whom He supersedes.

Other passages in Daniel lead us to believe that for him events in history were the counterparts of real processes in the supernatural world. The seer was able to discern, in symbolic forms, these supra-historical processes, and so to predict historical events in which they would ultimately be embodied. It remains that the Son of Man in the vision is a symbolic figure, and the fulfilment of the symbol is looked for within history. In what sense, then, did Jesus cite the prediction from Daniel?[14] It is gratuitous to assume that He must have interpreted it with strict literalness. I shall return to this question later (see pp. 80-83.)

There is another passage in Mark in which Jesus seems to predict the "coming" of the Son of Man: "Whoever is ashamed of me and mine[15] in this adulterous and sinful

[14] It is usual to assume that the Enochic doctrine of the Son of Man (Enoch xxxvii-lxxi) is presupposed in the teaching of Jesus, and that we should find here the clue to the sense in which the Danielic prophecy is to be understood. But (i) the last word has not been said about the integrity of the Similitudes of Enoch, or upon the date of the "Son of Man" passages, which are not found in any of the extant portions of the Greek Enoch, and have not been identified among the fairly copious Enochic material in the "Dead Sea Scrolls" (so far published); (ii) in spite of Otto's impressive argument (*Reich Gottes und Menschensohn*, pp. 141-189) I am not convinced of the influence of the Similitudes upon the teaching of Jesus in its earlier tradition (as distinct from their influence upon the growing eschatology of the Church); (iii) in any case Jesus explicitly refers to Daniel and not to Enoch; and (iv) He was at least as capable as the author of the Similitudes of giving His own re-interpretation (as that author does) of the Danielic symbolism; and the re-interpretation is likely to be highly original in view of the fact that His teaching disrupts the traditional eschatological scheme at a decisive point.

[15] The majority of MSS. read ἐμέ καὶ τοὺς ἐμοὺς λόγους. W and the Old Latin k omit λόγους, as do Western authorities in the parallel passage of Luke. C. H. Turner (*Mark* in *A New Commentary on Holy Scripture*, edited by Gore, Goudge and Guillaume) inclines to accept the shorter reading, which fits in admirably with such sayings as Mk. ix. 37; Mt. x. 40 = Lk. x. 16; Mt. xxv. 40, 45.

generation the Son of Man will be ashamed of him when he comes in the glory of his Father with the holy angels" (Mk. viii. 38). A similar saying occurred in "Q," as represented in Mt. x. 32-33 = Lk. xii 8-9.

MATTHEW	LUKE
"Everyone who acknowledges me before men, I will acknowledge him before my Father in heaven; but whoever denies me before men, I will deny him before my Father in heaven."	"Everyone who acknowledges me before men, the Son of Man will acknowledge him before the angels of God; but he who denies me before men will be denied before the angels of God."

Mark apparently has given only one member of a double saying in parallelism. This Hebraic parallelism is so characteristic of the sayings of Jesus, as of the prophetic tradition in which He stood, that we must suppose that the "Q" form (if we could recover it) was nearer to the original. Now in this form, the reference to the Son of Man is not so securely attested. It does not occur at all in Matthew, and in Luke it is confined to the positive member of the parallel, being omitted in the negative. In neither is there any reference to the "coming" of the Son of Man. Men will be confessed either "before my Father in heaven" or "before the angels of God."[16] That might or might not refer to a Day of Judgment closing history; but its most natural meaning is that Jesus (or the Son of Man) will acknowledge or deny men in the supernal world; that is, the acknowledgment or denial is eternal in quality.[17]

[16] "Before the angels of God" is an expression congenial to Luke (cf. xv. 10). "My Father in heaven" is equally characteristic of Matthew. We have no means of determining the wording of "Q." As Mark has both the Father and the angels we are still left in doubt which form of expression is more original. The meaning of both is the same. It is the same as "in heaven" (Lk. xv. 7).

[17] For a similar mode of expression, cf. Mt. xvi. 19, xviii. 18: "Whatever you forbid on earth will stand forbidden in heaven; and whatever you permit on earth will stand permitted in heaven"; that is, the inspired decisions of the apostles have eternal validity. By analogy, the meaning of the saying we are discussing would be that

It is not clear therefore that the saying originally conveyed an explicit prediction of the "coming" of the Son of Man. It is noteworthy that Matthew has not been content with the allusive reference to the "Coming" in Mark, but has recast the saying: "The Son of Man is to come in the glory of his Father with his angels, and then he will requite every-one according to what he has done." A comparison of "Q", Mark and Matthew seems to show a growing tendency to give precise "apocalyptic" form to a saying of Jesus, and of this tendency we have always to be aware in attempting to inter-pret the sayings.

We may usefully return at this point to the "Q" saying about the judging of the tribes, which we decided to ex-clude from the historical series of predictions. In its two versions it runs as follows:

MT. XIX. 28	LK. XXII. 28-30
"I tell you truly that you who followed me, at the Re-birth, when the Son of Man sits upon the throne of his glory, will sit, yourselves also, upon twelve thrones, judging the twelve tribes of Israel."	"It is you who have stood by me in my trials; and I assign to you, as my Father assigned to me a kingdom, that you shall eat and drink at my table in my kingdom, and sit upon thrones judging the twelve tribes of Israel."

It seems doubtful whether a common written source under-lies the two forms. The saying may have undergone develop-ment along two lines of oral tradition before reaching the evangelists, and its original form is hard to determine. But it clearly indicates the closest possible association of the disciples with their Lord in his coming glory as in His present tribu-lations. It is a companion to the other saying according to which those who acknowledge Him on earth will be acknow-ledged by Him in heaven. We may recall that in Daniel the Son of Man is "the people of the saints of the Most High." Although the Son of Man is now identified with Jesus Himself,

those who acknowledge Christ on earth thereby possess the sign that they are eternally accepted by Him.

so much of the earlier idea persists, that His followers are associated with Him in His reign. That the scene of that reign is placed in the transcendent order is explicit in Matthew alone, but it would seem to be the true intention of the saying in its Lucan form also. The "table" at which the disciples are to "eat and drink" recalls the "new wine" which Jesus is to drink "in the Kingdom of God," as well as the feast of the blessed "with Abraham, Isaac and Jacob in the Kingdom of heaven."

It is doubtful, then, whether the earlier tradition contained explicit predictions of an historical second coming of Jesus as Son of Man, though there are passages which refer to such a "coming" beyond history. There are, however, several other passages which predict that He, as Son of Man, will rise from the dead. The Marcan predictions of the Passion (viii. 31, ix. 31, x. 34) all culminate in an assurance of resurrection "after three days" (for which our other Synoptics give "on the third day," in accordance with the formula cited by Paul in I Cor. xv. 4). For those who deem the predictions of the Passion unhistorical, the prediction of the Resurrection is so *a fortiori*. I have freely admitted that the precise formulation of the predictons may be secondary, but I have shown reason for believing that Jesus did in fact forecast suffering and death for Himself. If so, is it to be believed that this was His last word about His fate?

It is true that in some forms of Jewish expectation the Messiah was destined to die. But our evidence for this is subsequent to the period of the Gospels; and in any case the Messiah does not die until He has reigned in glory. But Jesus had not yet reigned in glory. In the immediate prospect of death. He predicted that the Son of Man should be seen on the clouds of heaven. Whatever this was intended to symbolize, it is quoted from a vision of triumph, and could not be held to be fulfilled in the ignominious death of Jesus, as such. If therefore He did designate Himself as Son of Man, He must have expected that He would be victorious after death. It is therefore credible that He predicted not only His death but also His resurrection. It is noteworthy that nearly all of these predictions in Mark are of the form, "*The Son of Man* will suffer, die and rise again." There is only one saying

in which the first personal pronoun is used. Mk. xiv. 28:
"After I have been raised, I will precede you into Galilee"
(reported again by the "young man in white" at the sepulchre,
Mk. xvi. 7). The term "The Son of Man" is in its associations eschatological. Its use in these predictions seems to
indicate that both the death and the resurrection of Jesus are
"eschatological" events.

What then is the relation between the resurrection of the
Son of Man and His "coming"? First, we must observe
that according to Mk. xiv. 62 the Son of Man is to be seen
(a) "on the right hand of the Power," and (b) "coming
with the clouds of heaven." In the N.T. outside the Gospels
the "coming with the clouds" is still future, but the session
on the right hand of God is already attained: That is to
say, the Church, in the light of its own experience, has
divided the prediction of Mk. xiv. 62 into two stages.

Further, except in the Acts of the Apostles, no distinction
is drawn between the exaltation to the right hand of God,
and the resurrection[18]; or at least, there is no hint of any
interval between the two. Paul it appears, "saw the Lord"
in glory, "at the right hand of God" (I Cor. xv. 8, II Cor. iv. 6,
Rom. viii. 34). As he makes no distinction between his own
experience and that of Cephas and the rest, he appears to
assume that they too "saw the Lord" in glory. The theory
of forty days' interval between the resurrection and the ascension, with the prediction of a future descent "in like manner,"[19]
seems to be the product of a course of development within the
Church. The developed theory allows for three stages: resurrection, exaltation, second advent; but there is some reason to
think that at an early stage the two former were not distinguished, and in the saying in Mk. xiv. 62 the two latter
are at least closely associated. It is possible that all three
are aspects of one idea?

The resurrection is regularly predicted "after three days,"
or "on the third day." It might be argued that this is due to
the experience of the disciples, who began to "see the Lord,"
according to the Gospels, on the Sunday after the crucifixion.

[18] That is to say if the "Western Text" of Lk. xxiv. 51 is regarded
as original, as it probably should be.
[19] Acts i. 9-11.

But in the early formula cited by Paul in I Cor. xv. 3-7 the resurrection "on the third day" does not seem to be affirmed on the evidence of eye-witnesses, as are the appearances of the risen Lord.[20] It is "according to the Scriptures." What scriptures, Paul does not tell us. He no doubt took over the formula just as it was. The only O.T. passage which suggests itself is Hos. vi. 2: "After two days will he revive us; on the third day he will raise us up, and we shall live before him.[21] It looks as though the prophecy of the restoration of Israel, that is, the Day of the Lord, had been taken as a prophecy of the Day of the Son of Man (which would be quite in accord with the general line by which prophecy passed through apocalyptic into the thought of primitive Christianity), and the "third day," as a mysterious indication of the divinely-appointed term for that event. But we observe that the "three days" recur in the saying about the destruction and restoration of the temple. That raises the question, whether the use of Hosea's prophecy in this way may not go back to Jesus Himself[22] Might we go so far as to say that the "third day" is the Day of the Son of Man?[23]

[20] While the N.T. writers generally represent the death and the resurrection of Jesus quite naïvely as two distinct events in history, one of which happened three (or two) days after the other, there are traces of a different view. Thus, according to I Peter iii. 18, Jesus was "put to death in the flesh, but brought to life in the spirit"; the obverse and reverse of the same fact. According to Heb. ix. 11-14, the death of Christ, who "offered Himself to God through eternal Spirit", is also His entrance into the ultimate Sanctuary in the world of supreme reality (cf. ix. 24-28). For His death is itself an expression of pure obedience to the sovereign will of God (x. 9), and consequently it is the highest form of activity possible to any reasonable spirit. And finally, in the Fourth Gospel the death of Christ *is* His glorification, and not a preliminary to it.

[21] This passage was interpreted by Rabbis with reference to the general resurrection at the End of all things. See passages cited by Strack-Billerbeck on Mt. xvi. 21.

[22] Have we in Lk. xiii. 32-33 another adaptation of the Hosean formula? The realistic reference to Herod in this passage inclines one to regard the saying as authentic, not the less so because the situation implied is extremely difficult to fit into the familiar Marcan framework of the ministry. Again, there may be something after all in the view of the Fourth Evangelist that the saying about raising the temple in three days referred to the resurrection.

[23] If all this is not wholly fantastic, it would appear that the resurrection may be regarded as falling either into the "historical" or into

It is no more than a speculative conjecture, but one which has some probability on its side, that Jesus predicted, in terms which we cannot precisely recover, His own survival of death, and the ultimate triumph of the cause of God in His person; and that the Church interpreted Him in the light of its own experience.[24] Some of these predictions it expressed as a forecast of the resurrection of Jesus, as His followers had experienced it in the early days. Others it expressed in terms of His return " on the clouds of heaven," bringing the " Day of the Son of Man," conceived in apocalyptic fashion. Where He had referred to one single event, they made a distinction between two events, one past, His resurrection from the dead, and one future, His coming on the clouds. His other predictions were distributed (and sometimes differently in different strains of tradition) through the period expected to elapse between His death and His second coming. Thus the eschatological scheme of primitive Christianity was constructed.

There is nothing conclusive about such conjectures. They are invited by the obscurity of the actual *data*. The " apocalyptic " predictions, unlike those which refer to coming historical events, elude any precise formulation. It seems clear

the " apocalyptic " series of predictions. In so far as the predictions of resurrection fall together with those of the Day of the Son of Man, the resurrection is a symbol of the glory of Christ on the eternal plane. But in fact, something did happen on the historical plane corresponding to those predictions: possibly the event reflected in the stories of the empty tomb (which, as I think, are already implied in I Cor. xv); and in any case that series of experiences, which Paul could date in time, in which the early Christians " saw the Lord," and which had momentous effects in their lives, and for history, since out of them the Church emerged. It is highly suggestive that for Paul the resurrection of Christ marks the moment in history at which the new age began, and the eschatological hope came true.

[24] It appears to have been first made by Weiffenbach in 1873. See Schweitzer, *Leben-Jesu-Forschung*, 1913, pp. 227-229, 243. It is noteworthy that there is no saying which predicts both resurrection and second coming. It is therefore at least possible that the two are alternatives. The most difficult passage for this theory is Mk. xiv. 28, according to which Jesus is to rise from the dead in Jerusalem (presumably) and to make His way to Galilee; that is to say, the resurrection is an historical event in a sense in which the second coming cannot be, for of the latter no one can say " Lo here!" or " Lo there!"

that they have been in a special way subject to re-interpretation in terms of the developing eschatology of the early Church, and to recover their original form, or to determine their original intention, is a matter of extreme difficulty. It does appear that Jesus spoke in terms of current apocalypse of a " divine event," in which He would Himself appear in glory as Son of Man. With this event He seems to have associated the idea of a last judgment upon the quick and the dead, and of blessedness for His followers in a new Jerusalem with a temple " not made with hands." It is clearly not an historical event in any sense which we can attach to the term. If it is related to the historical series at all, it represents the point at which that series comes to an end. Matthew spoke of it as " Thy advent and the consummation of the age " (xxiv. 3).[25] He alone, however, of the evangelists is so explicit.

If then it is an event related in this way to history, what length of time is supposed to elapse between the ministry of Jesus and the close of history? Here our documents leave us in doubt. According to the eschatological scheme of Mk. xiii, the violation of the temple leads to a short and sharp tribulation in Judæa, and then comes the end,[26] before the generation to which Jesus spoke has died out.

But we have some reason to suppose that the disasters to fall upon the Jews were conceived by Jesus Himself as much more immediately impending. Are we then to say that He also conceived the Day of the Son of Man as much nearer than Mark reports it? It would seem so, if the saying addressed to the High Priest is to be interpreted literally at all. " You will see the Son of Man on the right hand of the Power and coming with the clouds of heaven." That assurance is offered in explication and in support of the claim to be the Messiah. It can hardly have been thought of as an event still in the remote future, for it is to be a sign to those persons, the members of the Sanhedrin, who were at that moment sitting in judgment upon the claim, and both Matthew and Luke have added to the saying words which show that they

[25] Both terms, παρουσία and συντέλεια τοῦ αἰῶνος are peculiar to Matthew among the evangelists.
[26] Mk. xiii. 24-27.

understood it to refer to something beginning "from this moment."[27]

Consider again the reference to "three days" in the predictions of resurrection and of the restoration of the temple. I have tried to show that both these predictions belong to the "apocalyptic" series, and point to the Day of the Son of Man. The formula of "the third day" was clearly intended by Hosea to suggest that *speedy* restoration of Israel. Its adoption by Jesus would naturally be supposed to carry a similar suggestion of the speedy approach of the Day of the Son of Man.

If then these "apocalyptic" predictions are to be understood literally, they seem to point to an event expected to happen very soon indeed, and this is the view commonly taken by those who adopt the "eschatological" interpretation of the Gospels. But, as they clearly see, this raises a difficulty in regard to the ethical teaching of Jesus. Some of them have attempted to represent this ethical teaching as "interim ethics," in the sense of precepts for the life of the disciples during the very short interval before normal conditions of human life cease to be. But it has become clear that the sayings cannot be convincingly interpreted in this sense. The alternative would seem to be to regard almost all the ethical precepts attributed to Jesus as the deposit of the teaching given by the Church to its members in the early years, and this view finds much favour at present.[28] That the original tradition of the teaching of Jesus has undergone some expansion for the purposes of moral instruction in the Church becomes certain from a comparison of the Gospels; but to eliminate ethical precepts from the tradition of the teaching of Jesus is an

---

[27] Mt., ἀπ' ἄρτι, Lk. ἀπὸ τοῦ νῦν. Observe, however, that in Luke the coming with clouds is not mentioned. It is the session at God's right hand that is immediately impending (ἀπὸ τοῦ νῦν ἔσται). This accords with the normal view of the early Church: Christ *is* at the right hand of God; he *will* come in glory. In Matthew, however, the session and the coming are conjoined, and *both* are to be seen immediately (ἀπ' ἄρτι ὄψεσθε).

[28] It is represented in its extreme form by Rudolf Bultmann, see *Geschichte der synoptischen Tradition*, 1931, pp. 73-160. It may be regarded as an exaggerated reaction from the "liberal" view of Jesus as a moral teacher and nothing more.

heroic piece of destructive criticism to which we should do well not to commit ourselves too rashly.

We seem to be confronted with two diverse strains in the teaching of Jesus, one of which appears to contemplate the indefinite continuance of human life under historical conditions, while the other appears to suggest a speedy end to these conditions. A drastic criticism might eliminate the one strain or the other, but both are deeply embedded in the earliest form of tradition known to us. It would be better to admit that we do not possess the key to their reconciliation than to do such violence to our documents.

It may be possible to find a place for both strains if we make full allowance for the symbolic character of the "apocalyptic" sayings. The symbolic method is inherent in apocalyptic. The course of history, past, present and future, with its climax in the Day of the Lord, is presented in a series of symbolic visions. So far as the apocalyptists use this method to describe history down to their own time, the interpretation is plain, because we have before us, as they had, the actual events corresponding to the images employed, and they sometimes supply the key. But when they come to describe the supposed future course of history, there is no actuality within our experience, or theirs, corresponding to the imagery. How far did these writers suppose the images themselves to be actuality? The answer to the question would no doubt be different for different writers. For the author of the Book of Daniel, for example, the actuality corresponding to the victory of the "Son of Man" over the "beasts" is a victory of the Jews over the Seleucid monarchy, and the subsequent erection of a Jewish empire.[29] It had not happened when he wrote, but it had for him the actuality of an impending historical event.

There are, however, writers who certainly seem to be de-

[29] I do not mean to say that there is nothing "supernatural" in the predictions of "Daniel." No doubt he may have conceived the victory as brought about miraculously, and the subsequent kingdom of the saints is certainly painted in supernatural colours. But there can be no doubt that the seer expected to experience, with his contemporaries, the events I have mentioned, on the plane of history.

scribing, in their own intention, that which lies beyond history altogether. Must we assume that they always intended their visions of the end, unlike their visions of coming events within history, to be taken with the strictest literalness, or does a consciously symbolic element still persist? How can we tell what was in their minds? It does however seem probable that the more deeply spiritual their outlook was, the more clearly they must have been aware that the ultimate reality lies beyond anything that the mind of man can conceive, and that any form in which he can imagine it must remain strictly symbolic. It is at least open to the reader to take the traditional apocalyptic imagery as a series of symbols standing for realities which the human mind cannot directly apprehend, and as such capable of various interpretation and re-interpretation as the lessons of history or a deepening understanding of the ways of God demand.

Now in the teaching of Jesus the traditional apocalyptic symbolism is controlled by the central idea of the Kingdom of God. This idea was itself an element in the eschatological complex with which the apocalyptists worked, though in their writings it is less prominent than other ideas of the same order. But it is peculiarly fitted to express the essential religious conviction which underlies, and which alone can justify, the eschatological hope in all its aspects. Judgment and unending bliss, the establishment of righteousness, the perfecting of human nature and the renovation of the universe, are *religious* ideas only so far as they depend on the conviction that the Lord is King, and that His will is the ultimate good which the whole created universe is destined to realize. It is therefore significant that the idea of the Kingdom of God has a central and controlling position in the teaching of Jesus which it has in no other body of religious teaching. With it are associated the traditional symbols for judgment and bliss, and, as the bearer and representative of the Kingdom, the traditional and symbolic figure of the Son of Man. All these are "eschatological" in character; they are ultimates, and are proper not to this empirical realm of time and space, but to the absolute order.

But Jesus declares that this ultimate, the Kingdom of God, has come into history, and He takes upon Himself the

" eschatological " role of " Son of Man." The absolute, the " wholly other," has entered into time and space. And as the Kingdom of God has come and the Son of Man has come, so also judgment and blessedness have come into human experience. The ancient images of the heavenly feast; of Doomsday, of the Son of Man at the right hand of power, are not only symbols of supra-sensible, supra-historical realities; they have also their corresponding actuality within history. Thus both the facts of the life of Jesus, and the events which He foretells within the historical order, are " eschatological " events, for they fall within the coming of the Kingdom of God. In particular, the death and resurrection of Jesus Christ possess a unique significance which is hinted at by the use of apocalyptic symbolism. To go back to Daniel, the symbolic vision discloses to the prophetic eye a reality of the supernal world, the ultimate triumph of the cause of God over all hostile powers, and this has its counterpart in a parallel sequence of events on earth, conceived as immediately impending. On analogy, in Mark. xiv. 62 the coming of the Son of Man with clouds, standing, as in Daniel, for the ultimate triumph of the cause of God, should have its historical counterpart in events immediately impending (as is implied in the language of the Gospels), and these can hardly be other than the sacrificial death and resurrection of Christ. This is, on the historical plane, the triumph of the cause of God, the coming of the Son of Man.[30] The historical order however cannot contain the whole meaning of the absolute. The imagery therefore retains its significance as symbolizing the eternal realities, which though they enter into history are never exhausted in it. The Son of Man has come, but also He will come[31], the sin of men is judged, but also it will be judged.

But these future tenses are only an accommodation of language. There is no coming of the Son of Man in history " after " His coming in Galilee and Jerusalem, whether soon or late, for there is no before and after in the eternal order.

[30] Similarly J. A. T. Robinson (now Bishop of Woolwich) *Jesus and His Coming* (S.C.M. Press, 1957) pp. 43-52.
[31] In Lk. xvii. 22, " the days of the Son of Man " seems to refer to His ministry on earth, while the same phrase in xvii. 26 refers to His advent in glory.

The Kingdom of God in its full reality is not something which will happen after other things have happened. It is that to which men awake when this order of time and space no longer limits their vision, when they " sit at meat in the Kingdom of God " with all the blessed dead, and drink with Christ the " new wine " of eternal felicity. " The Day of the Son of Man " stands for the timeless fact. So far as history can contain it, it is embodied in the historic crisis which the coming of Jesus brought about. But the spirit of man, though dwelling in history, belongs to the eternal order, and the full meaning of the Day of the Son of Man, or the Kingdom of God, he can experience only in that eternal order. That which cannot be experienced in history is symbolized by the picture of a coming event, and its timeless quality is expressed as pure simultaneity in time—" as the lightning flashes."

The predictions of Jesus have no long historical perspective. They seem to be concerned with the immediate developments of the crisis which was already in being when He spoke, and which He interpreted as the coming of the Kingdom of God. But this does not necessarily mean (if the view I have set forth is admissible) that He believed that history would come to an end shortly after His death. The eternal significance of history had revealed itself in this crisis. Whether its subsequent span would be long or short, men would henceforth be living in a new age, in which the Kingdom of God, His grace and His judgment, stood revealed. Hence there is a place for ethical teaching, not as " interim ethics," but as a moral ideal for men who have " accepted the Kingdom of God," and live their lives in the presence of His judgment and His grace, now decisively revealed.

The experience of many generations has no doubt brought a growing understanding of the meaning of that revelation, and the attempts to live by the ethical teaching of Jesus has had results in history. We may hope yet to understand Him better, and to see His ethical principles more fully embodied in our social life. But of all this we hear nothing in His sayings. He points His hearers directly from the historic crisis in which they were involved to the eternal order of which that crisis was a mirror.

It is to some such view that we seem to be led in the

attempt to find in the teaching of Jesus the unity and consistency which it must have possessed. We have however so far dealt only with those sayings which are more or less explicit, even though making use of symbolism. But a great deal of the teaching on precisely these themes is contained in parables. The theory which I have enunciated may be regarded as an hypothesis to be tested by applying it to the interpretation of the parables, some of which, as currently interpreted, seem to point to a period, long or short, during which the disciples of Christ are to wait for His second coming, and during which the Kingdom of God " grows " on earth.

Chapter IV

THE SETTING IN LIFE

The most recent school of Gospel criticism, that of *Form-geschichte,* or "Form-criticism," has taught us that in order to understand rightly any passage in the Gospels we must enquire into the "setting in life" (*Sitz im leben*) in which the tradition underlying that passage took form. The original "setting in life" of any authentic saying of Jesus was of course provided by the actual conditions of His ministry. But the form-critics rightly call our attention to the fact that the formed tradition of His teaching, as it reaches us, has often been affected by the changed conditions under which His followers lived during the period between His death and the completion of our Gospels. Its "setting in life" is provided by the situation in the early Church. It is important to bear this distinction in mind in studying the parables. We shall sometimes have to remove a parable from its setting in the life and thought of the Church, as represented by the Gospels, and make an attempt to reconstruct its original setting in the life of Jesus.

There are, however, a number of parables whose bearing upon the situation that existed during the ministry of Jesus is clear enough in the Gospels as they stand. Some of these I shall consider first.

Among the parables explicitly referred to the Kingdom of God, two of the shortest and simplest are those of the Hid Treasure and the Costly Pearl, which form a pair in Mt. xiii. 44-46. In each of them we have a picture of a man suddenly confronted with a treasure of inestimable worth, which he forthwith acquires at the cost of all that he has.[1] For their

[1] Jülicher (*Gleichnisreden Jesu,* II, 1910, pp. 581-585) has sufficiently shown how impossible it is to allegorize the details, and how aptly they are chosen to depict, with the greatest possible economy of language, a realistic situation. If we attempt to draw "morals" from the details, we get into difficulties. The finder of the treasure hides it

interpretation the only real question that arises is whether the
tertium companationis is the immense value of the thing
found, or the sacrifice by which it is acquired. This question
is, I think, decided by the following considerations. First,
inasmuch as the Kingdom of God was conceived by those whom
Jesus addressed as the great object of hope and prayer, they
did not need to be assured of its value. Secondly, the parables,
like the majority of the parables of Jesus, set forth an example
of human action, and invite a judgment upon it. Was the
peasant a fool to impoverish himself for the sake of buying
the field? Was it unpardonable rashnes in the merchant
to realize all his assets to buy a single pearl? At first sight,
yes. But to know when to plunge makes the successful finan-
cier. Only, you must feel quite sure of the value of the property
you are buying.

What then is the "setting in life"? The Matthæan context gives no real help. The "parabolic discourse" of Mt. xiii.
is clearly made up by expanding the corresponding discourse
of Mk. iv with material drawn from other sources; and the
Marcan discourse itself has long been recognized as a compilation. We have to conjecture a situation in which the
idea of great sacrifices for a worthy end is prominent. There
is no difficulty in finding such a situation. In Mk. x. 17-30,
and other kindred passages, Jesus is represented as calling
for volunteers to join a cause. It may mean leaving home
and friends, property and business; it may mean a vagrant
life of hardship, with an ignominious death at the end. Is
it folly to join such a losing cause? The parables before us
fit such a situation. They are not intended to illustrate any
general maxim, but to enforce an appeal which Jesus was
making for a specific course of action then and there. The
implicit argument they contained is cogent, provided that
the Kingdom of God is in some way identified with the
cause of Jesus. They do not indeed indicate whether the pos-
session of the Kingdom is immediate or in prospect. But
with the fundamental principle in mind, that Jesus saw in
His own ministry the coming of the Kingdom of God, we

---

again, so that the owner shall not get wind of his find, and then bids
for the property, presumably at its market value as agricultural land.
He is as unscrupulous in his way as the Unjust Steward himself.

may state the argument thus: You agree that the Kingdom of God is the highest good: it is within your power to possess it here and now,[2] if, like the treasure-finder and the pearl-merchant, you will throw caution to the winds: "Follow me!"

If now in other parables, which are not directly applied to the Kingdom of God, we find a reference to the same aspect of the ministry of Jesus, we can hardly be wrong in treating them as being, in the same sense, "parables of the Kingdom." Such, for example, are the twin parables of the Tower-builder and the King going to War (Lk. xiv. 28-33). These are associated by the evangelist with the call of Jesus to men to take great risks with open eyes; and although the actual connection in which he has placed them may be artificial, the general reference is no doubt right. The parables may be aptly illustrated by the episodes related in Mt. viii. 19-22, Lk. ix. 57-62, where possible followers are reminded in stern terms of the cost which they must be prepared to pay.

Take again the parable of the Children in the Market-place, which, as we have seen, comes down to us with an application to the frivolous attitude of the Jewish public to the work of Jesus and of John the Baptist alike. There is no good reason for doubting this application. If in the ministry of Jesus the Kingdom of God comes, as in the ministry of John its coming had been heralded, then our attention is drawn to the egregious folly of such childish behaviour in the presence of the supreme crisis of history. There is indeed no reference to the Kingdom of God, but the words, "the Son of Man came," echo the language of eschatology.[3] The coming of the Son of Man is the coming of the Kingdom of

[2] This is perhaps what is meant by the ἐντὸς ὑμῶν of Lk. xvii. 21, see p. 62 n. 4.

[3] If, however, the expression "the Son of Man" is original here, we should have to suppose either (a) that the saying was addressed not to the general public but to a circle already prepared to accept Jesus as "Son of Man"; or (b) that the term "the Son of Man" was an ambiguous one, which did not necessarily carry its specific "eschatological" meaning to the general public. Whether or not the term "the Son of Man" was actually used by Jesus in this saying, it was present in the earliest form of the tradition accessible to us, and it is congruous with the "eschatological" significance which Jesus attributed to His own ministry.

God. In the light of this we might perhaps interpret the cryptic words with which the passage closes. If the Matthæan form is original, "Wisdom is justified by her works," the meaning may be that the actual facts of the present situation, however it may be misjudged by the frivolous minded, demonstrate the wisdom and righteousness of God, that is, they are the manifestation of His "Kingdom." But since Luke gives a different form (" Wisdom is justified by all her children ") we cannot be sure of the original sense.

In Mk. ii. 18-19 we have a brief narrative, in which the disciples of Jesus are censured for not fasting, like the disciples of John and the Pharisees, and Jesus replies with a brief parabolic saying: " Can the groomsmen fast while the bridegroom is with them?" The allusion is to the custom by which the attendants upon a newly-married pair were released from certain religious duties during the seven days of the wedding festivities, in order that the rejoicings might not be interrupted. The saying therefore depicts in brief a familiar situation and asks for a judgment upon it. The application is indicated by the setting which the evangelist has given in the introductory narrative, and there is no serious reason to question it.[4] It would be as unreasonable to require the disciples of Jesus to fast, as it is admittedly unreasonable to expect wedding-guests to do so. Clearly then the disciples are conceived to be in a situation to which joy and not grief is appropriate. We recall such sayings as " Blessed are your eyes, for they see "; " Blessed are ye poor, for yours is the Kingdom of God." For those who have " accepted the Kingdom of God as a little child," there is pure happiness which makes any such rite as penitential fasting a mockery. For the Kingdom of God is, in a familiar figure, a feast of the blessed.[5]

[4] The passage is one of those styled by Dibelius " paradigms " (*From Tradition to Gospel*, p. 43), and he regards the " paradigms " as the most surely authentic part of the narrative tradition. From a different point of view Albertz (*Die synoptischen Streitgespräche*, pp. 57-64) gives weighty reasons for regarding this and other " controversial " episodes in Mark as " material of uncommon value historically."

[5] It is reasonably suspected by many critics that the continuation of the parable in Mk. ii. 20 is a secondary development. There can be little doubt that readers of the Gospel would understand it to mean that although Jesus had set aside fasting during His lifetime, the Church

To this controversy about fasting Mark has appended a pair of parables, those of the Patched Garment and the Old Wineskins. In the intention of the evangelist at least they have an application similar to that of the parable we have just considered. Their common motive is the folly of trying to accommodate the old and the new. The ministry of Jesus is not to be regarded as an attempt to reform Judaism; it brings something entirely new, which cannot be accommodated to the traditional system. In other words, "The law and the prophets were until John; from his time the Kingdom of God is proclaimed."

Let us now consider in the same way another group of parables, beginning with the short parabolic saying, "It is not the healthy who need the physician, but the sick" (Mk. ii. 17). The evangelist has supplied both a narrative setting and a "moral." The narrative relates how Jesus called Levi the publican, and subsequently dined in company with many "publicans and sinners." This brought an expostulation from the scribes, and the parable was the reply. The "moral," "I did not come to call righteous people, but sinners" is appropriate to the "calling" of Levi with which the story starts. It is not, however, particularly apt to the question, "Why does he eat with publicans and sinners?" Moreover, it raises a notorious difficulty about the use of the term "righteous." Did Jesus really say that His mission was to sinners and *not* to the righteous? Was righteousness a positive disqualification for

---

was justified in resuming the practice after His death. This implies that the "bridegroom" of the story is Jesus Himself (cf. Rev. xix. 7, xxi. 9; II Cor. xi. 2), and so the parable becomes an allegory. This allegorization was probably not originally intended. If the parable meant, as I have suggested, that the disciples enjoy pure happiness because they are "in the Kingdom of God," then it is impossible to suppose that the time for rejoicing will soon pass, and the time for fasting return; for the Kingdom of God endures. In the parable, "while the bridegroom is with them," means "during the marriage festivities." If ii. 20 was an original part of it, it can only have been intended to suggest, in characteristic antithetical style, the exceptional character of the festival period; during the festivities, and only then, fasting is out of place. For a suggestive interpretation of the disappearance of the bridegroom, see Cadoux, *op. cit.*, pp. 72 sqq. I do not, however, find it convincing, and it ignores the equivalence of the feast, in imagery, with the Kingdom of God.

discipleship? In view of Mk. x. 17-21 it hardly seems likely. Then is the term "righteous" used with bitter irony ("those who had confidence in themselves that they were righteous and despised others" Lk. xviii. 9)? If so, it is not an appropriate interpretation of the "healthy" of the parable.

In short, we may fairly suspect that the "moral" is no part of the original saying, but a rough interpretation of the parable on allegorical lines. "It is not the healthy who need a physician, but the sick": "healthy"=righteous; "sick"=sinners; "physician"=Jesus. Whether or not the narrative setting is as original as the parable itself we need not discuss,[6] but there is no reason to doubt that the saying was intended to be applied to some such situation. The friendship of Jesus with "publicans and sinners" we have already found referred to in the parable of the Children in the Market-place. It is unquestionably one of the features of His ministry which attracted most attention and most criticism. That "sick folk need a doctor" is obviously an apt reply to such criticisms.

Luke (ch. xv.) has used a similar setting for the three parables of the Lost Sheep, Lost Coin and Prodigal Son, of which the first two form a characteristic pair, while the third is related in subject, but different in treatment. The Lost Sheep (though not its companion parable) occurs also, in a different setting, in Matthew (xviii. 12-14). Both evangelists give a "moral." In Luke it runs, "I tell you that in the same way there is joy in heaven over one sinner who repents, more than over ninety-nine righteous persons who do not need repentance"; in Matthew, "In the same way it is not the will of your Father in heaven that one of these little ones should perish." Both cannot be original; possibly neither is. The Lucan "moral" keeps more closely to the terms of the parable itself, but the reference to the "righteous" is open to the objection which arose in regard to Mk. ii. 17 (did Jesus really teach that there were righteous persons who needed no repentance?); and there is the same suggestion of allegory: home-keeping sheep=righteous persons; strayed sheep=

---

[6] Dibelius (*op. cit.*, p. 61) recognizes the call of Levi as an authentic "paradigm," and supposes that the parable originally belonged to it; the scene of the feast with publican and sinners was composed by the evangelist. His argument does not seem to me particularly cogent.

sinners; strayed sheep found= repentant sinner; hence, 1 repentant sinner is better than 99 righteous persons. It is a little too mechanical.

Now the story itself (and the companion parable of the Lost Coin follows the same line)[7] depicts vividly the concern which a person feels about a loss which an outsider might consider comparatively trifling, and his (or her) corresponding delight when the lost is found. The Lucan setting is surely so far right, that the parables refer to the extravagant concern (as it seemed to some) which Jesus displayed for the depressed classes of the Jewish community.[8] We need not ask whether Jesus Himself, or God, is thought of as the Seeker of the lost. In the ministry of Jesus the Kingdom of God came; and one of the features of its coming was this unprecedented concern for the " lost."

The parable of the Prodigal Son is not exactly parallel with the other two. Its point would seem to lie in the contrast between the delight of a father at the return of his scapegrace son, and the churlish attitude of the " respectable " elder brother. The application, however, is to the same situation in the ministry of Jesus. So Luke represents it, and we cannot doubt that he is right.

This motive, of the contrast between those whom the evangelists call the " righteous " and " sinners " respectively, recurs in other parables. Thus the Matthæan parable of the Two Sons (Mt. xxi. 28-32)[9] is clearly a comment on the rejection of the word of God by the religious leaders, and its acceptance by the outcasts, as the evangelist represents it.

It finds more elaborate expression in the parable of the Great Feast (Mt. xxii. 1-13; Lk. xiv. 16-24). In Matthew, though not in Luke, the parable begins " The Kingdom of Heaven is like . . ." In Luke it is prefaced by the words " Blessed is he who shall eat bread in the Kingdom of God."

[7] The fact that the two parables are clearly directed to the same point debars us from finding the *primary* clue to their meaning in the relation of shepherd and sheep. At the same time, the hearers of the first parable could hardly fail to be reminded of the familiar O.T. imagery of Jehovah and His flock.

[8] And possibly for some inhabitants of Galilee who were not Jews? " Sinners of the Gentiles " (cf. Gal. ii. 15) lived cheek by jowl with Jews in that district.

[9] Quoted on pp. 11-12.

The difference between the two versions of the parable make it unlikely that the evangelists depended upon a single proximate source; but that they are following variant traditions of the identical story is clear. The common nucleus of the story tells how the invited guests were left out of the feast by their own act, and their places taken by rag-tag-and-bobtail. Now the symbol of the heavenly banquet was a traditional one for the bliss of the good time coming, when the Kingdom of God should be revealed. Jesus Himself employed this symbolism in other sayings.[10] The audience therefore might be expected to take the allusion. In that case, the words of invitation (common to both accounts, though with slight verbal differences): "Come, for all is ready," correspond to the call of Jesus, "Repent, for the Kingdom of God has come"; and the parable suggests the rejection of that call by the "righteous," and its acceptance by "publicans and sinners."

In the elaboration of the story by the two evangelists we may detect the interests of the Church at a later date. Luke has duplicated the episode of the last-minute invitations. First, messengers go into the "squares and alleys of the city" to collect guests; and since there are still vacant places, they are sent farther afield into the highways and hedges. It is probable, as most commentators hold, that Luke has here in view the extension of the Gospel to the Gentiles. Matthew, on the other hand, has only one set of last-minute invitations. He followed a tradition which was not interested in the calling of the Gentiles (cf. x. 5-6). But he has made the feast into a wedding feast for a king's son, a trait which was no doubt intended to be interpreted allegorically[11]; and he adds the episode of the man without a wedding-garment. This was perhaps in origin a separate parable, but Matthew seems to have intended to guard against the reception of the Gentiles into the Church on too easy terms.[12]

A similar motive underlies the Matthæan parable of the Labourers in the Vineyard (Mt. xx. 1-16), which again is introduced with the formula, "The Kingdom of Heaven is like . . ." Matthew has added at the close the saying "The

[10] See pp. 38-40.   [11] Further allegorical traits in xxii. 6-7.
[12] The attitude betrayed here, as in v. 17-19, x. 5-6, xxii. 2-3, seems to resemble that of the "Judaistic" opponents of Paul, as we infer it from his epistles.

last shall be first and first last." But this saying is found elsewhere in different contexts,[13] and has no obvious appropriateness in relation to the parable. The point of the story is that the employer, out of sheer generosity and compassion for the unemployed, pays as large a wage to those who have worked for one hour as to those who have worked all day. It is a striking picture of the divine generosity which gives without regard to the measures of strict justice. But its " setting in life " must surely be sought in the facts of the ministry of Jesus. The divine generosity was specifically exhibited in the calling of publicans and sinners who had no merit before God. The Kingdom of God is like that. Such is Jesus' retort to the complaints of the legally minded who cavilled at Him as the friend of publicans and sinners.

A further aspect of the ministry of Jesus is illustrated in the parable of the Strong Man Despoiled (Mk. iii. 27, Lk. xi. 21-22). In its Marcan form it runs :

" No one can enter the strong man's house and plunder his gear, unless he first binds the strong man; then he will plunder his house."

The Lucan version (which is probably drawn from a different source) is more elaborate. Instead of an ordinary case of burglary, we have a story about an armed man guarding his courtyard. He is attacked by an enemy superior in strength, who challenges him to combat, overcomes and disarms him, and then plunders his goods at leisure. We may think of a border incident on the frontiers of Syria, always exposed to Bedouin raids. The heightening of the picture we may put to the credit of the Greek evangelist. But the purpose of the story is the same. Now both Luke and Mark (followed by Matthew), associate this parable with the exorcisms of Jesus, in which He sees the end of Satan's kingdom. In the Jewish thought the end of the kingdom of Satan is associated with the coming of the Kingdom of God.[14]; and in fact both Matthew and Luke have given in the immediate context the saying, " If I by the finger [or Spirit] of God cast out demons,

---

[13] Mt. xix. 30, following Mk. x. 31; Lk. xiii. 30.
[14] See pp. 23-24.

then the Kingdom of God has come upon you." The evangelists therefore unanimously regard the parable of the Kingdom of God, in the sense that they apply the metaphor of the overthrow of the strong man to the defeat of the power of evil. And in this they are doubtless right. But for our present purpose it is important to observe that the defeat of the powers of evil is not, as in Jewish apocalyptic, a hope for the future, but something actually accomplished in the ministry of Jesus. Once again, the ministry of Jesus is an eschatological event. It is the coming of the Kingdom of God.

The most difficult of the parables referring directly to the existing situation is that of the Wicked Husbandmen (Mk. xii. 1-8[15]). For Jülicher[16] and his followers this is an allegory constructed by the early Church with the death of Jesus in retrospect. I cannot agree. As we shall see, there is reason to think that it has suffered a certain amount of expansion, but the story in its main lines is natural and realistic in every way.

An absentee landlord let off a vineyard to tenant cultivators. He made with them a contract stipulating for the payment of rent in the form of a proportion of the produce.[17] After vintage he sent his agents to demand his rent. But an absentee landlord is fair game if the tenants see their chance. They paid their rent in blows. The landlord, realizing that the situation was serious, sent his son to deal with it. The son of the proprietor would surely command a respect which was denied to the slaves who had represented him in the first instance. But the tenantry already had the bit between their teeth. They murdered the landlord's son, cast his body unburied outside the vineyard, and seized the property.

[15] Provisionally I put the end of the parable here, for reasons which will appear presently.

[16] *Gleichnisreden Jesu*, II, 1910, pp. 385-406. He admits the possibility that there may have existed a parable of Jesus about wicked husbandmen, traces of which may perhaps be recognized in xii. 1, 9, but " any attempt to reconstruct it is hopeless, since our only source, Mk. xii., is to be understood down to the last detail as a product of early Christian theology, and so much the less as an authentic report of a controversial discourse of Jesus."

[17] For examples of contracts stipulating for payment of rent in kind, see *Oxyrhynchus Papyri*, 1631, 1689, 1968. The practice was common.

The story has the more verisimilitude if we remember the conditions of the country at the time. Palestine, and Galilee in particular, was a disaffected region. Since the revolt of Judas the Gaulonite in A.D. 6 the country had never been altogether pacified. The unrest had in part economic causes.[18] If now we recall that large estates were often held by foreigners, we may well suppose that agrarian discontent went hand in hand with nationalist feeling, as it did in pre-war Ireland. We can then see that all the conditions were present under which refusal of rent might be the prelude to murder and the forcible seizure of land by the peasantry. The parable, in fact, so far from being an artificially constructed allegory, may be taken as evidence of the kind of thing that went on in Galilee during the half century preceding the general revolt of A.D. 66.

The parable closes, as a parable should, with a question: "What will the owner of the vineyard do?" (xii. 9). Well, everybody knew what was the end of such an affair, whether or not Jesus answered His own question (contrary to His custom), as Mark avers. The question, however, really means, "What did these men deserve?" The answer expected is that they deserve the worst, for their crime was such as every decent man must abhor.

What is the application? The opening words of the story are all but a quotation from Isaiah's Song of the Vineyard (Is. v. 1-2), which would be familiar to every Jewish hearer. Every such hearer would also know that by long tradition, beginning from that poem of Isaiah's, Israel was the Lord's vineyard. It follows that the crime of the wicked husbandmen, who refused their landlord his due, and met his appeals with defiance that stopped at nothing, is the crime of the rulers of Israel. Mark says that they recognized that the parable was aimed at them (xii. 12), and we can well believe it.

According to Mk. xii. 9, Jesus answered His own question: "He will come and destroy the cultivators, and will give the vineyards to others." in itself this is a natural conclusion to the story. When a mutinous tenantry had broken out into

[18] See F. C. Grant, *The Economic Background of the Gospels* (Oxford University Press, 1926).

open revolt, it was no doubt possible for the landlord to obtain assistance from the government to put it down by force[19]; and he would then look for new tenants. The general implication of the answer, moreover, is in harmony with the known teaching of Jesus. He did apparently foretell the disruption of the Jewish community. Nor do the terms of the answer correspond so precisely with historical events that they must be a *vaticinium ex eventu*. In the Christian view, indeed, religous leadership did pass from the Jewish authorities to the apostles of Christ; but the former were not " destroyed " until the Roman capture of Jerusalem, which was probably still in the future when Mark wrote. It appears, however, that it was not the practice of Jesus to answer the questions to which His parables so often lead up; and on the other hand it is the practice of the evangelists to point the moral of parables. It must therefore be regarded as uncertain whether xii. 9b is an integral part of the authentic tradition.

Matthew (xxi. 41) has restored the form more usual in the conclusion of parables, by making the audience answer the question: "He will evilly destroy the evil men and will let the vineyard to other cultivators, who will deliver the produce to him in its season "; and he makes Jesus enforce the application in explicit terms: "Therefore I tell you that the Kingdom of God will be taken away from you and given to a nation that brings forth its fruits." In the phrase " he will evilly destroy the evil men," we may reasonably see an allusion to the horrors of the Roman capture of Jerusalem: and in the concluding sentence we surely have the doctrine of the rejection of Israel and the election of the Gentiles, as it meets us in other parts of the N.T. The Church is dotting the i's and crossing the t's of the original application. In addition to the application of the parable, all three evangelists have appended a *testimonium* from the O.T. "The stone which the builders rejected has become the top of the

---

[19] Much as Marcus Brutus collected a debt from the corporation of Salamis by arranging for the dispatch of a force of cavalry obtained from the governor of Cilicia, with which his agent besieged the town council until five members died of starvation. See Cicero, *Ad Atticum*, V. 21, VI. 1, where the whole discreditable episode is described with a mordant pen.

corner " (Mk. xii. 10 and parallels), and Luke has added a further saying about a stone[20] which brings disaster upon those who fall on it and upon those on whom it falls (Lk. xx. 18).

All this progressive elaboration indicates that the Church held the parable to be of peculiar importance, and was anxious to put its interpretation beyond doubt.

This being so, it would not be surprising if the details of the story itself, even in its earlier canonical form, had suffered some measure of manipulation in order to point the moral more clearly. The parable as we have it in Mark invites an allegorical interpretation in which the " servants " stand for the prophets, and the " beloved son " for Jesus. How far is such an interpretation responsible for the actual terms of the story? There are two points upon which suspicion has particularly fallen.

First, the long series of " servants " sent by the landlord to claim his rent strikes the reader as unreal in the supposed situation. The number may well have been multiplied in order to suggest the long roll of prophets sent by God to His people and rejected or martyred by them. If we excised Mk. xii. 4, we should have a climactic series of three, which is congenial to this form of story (as to folktales)[21] : " He sent to the cultivators at the season a slave to receive from the cultivators (the amount due) from the produce of the vineyard; and they took and beat him and sent him away empty-handed. And again he sent to them another slave, and him they beheaded and outraged. He still had a favourite son. He sent him to them last of all." That reads naturally enough.[22]

[20] Behind this accumulation of passages from the Old Testament lies a traditional scheme of " testimonies." See my book, *According to the Scriptures* (Nisbet, 1952).

[21] Cf. the three servants in the parable of the Money on Trust, the three refusals in the (Lucan) parable of the Great Feast, and the Priest, Levite and Samaritan. The parables in story form have much in common with folk-tales.

[22] This simpler form is now actually to be found in a newly discovered text. See *The Gospel according to Thomas*: Coptic Text established and translated by A. Guillawmont and others (Collins, 1959) p. 39 (93-116). This tends so far to support the suggestion which has been made that this late Gnostic work draws in places upon a primitive tradition of the Sayings, though Grant and Freedman, in their commentary on it (*The Secret Sayings of Jesus according to the*

Secondly, it has been thought that the murder of the "beloved son" is too obvious a reflection of the theology of the early Church to be accepted as part of a genuine parable of Jesus. But we must observe that a climax of iniquity is demanded by the plot of the story. The outrageous contumacy of the tenants must be exhibited in the most emphatic way. How could it better be emphasized than by bringing on the scene the landlord's only,[23] or favourite, son? It is the logic of the story, and not any theological motive, that has introduced this figure. Moreover, the description of the murder of the son betrays no reminiscence of the manner of the death of Jesus. Matthew has in fact attempted to remedy this. He makes the tenants first expel the son from the vineyard and then kill him[24]—as Jesus "suffered without the gate" (Heb. xiii 12). But in the Marcan version there is not even this hint.

The parable therefore stands on its own feet as a dramatic story, inviting a judgment from the hearers, and the application of the judgment is clear enough without any allegorizing of the details. Nevertheless, the climax of iniquity in the story suggests a similar climax in the situation to which it is to be applied. We know that Jesus did regard His own ministry as the culmination of God's dealings with His people, and that He declared that the guilt of all righteous blood from Abel to Zechariah would fall upon that generation. Consequently the parable would suggest, by a kind of tragic irony, the impending climax of the rebellion of Israel in a murderous assault upon the Successor of the prophets. If now we concede that Mark has placed the parable in its true historical context (and in the Passion-narrative, to which this part of the Gospel

---

Gospel of Thomas, Fontana Books, Collins, 1960) hold that the "Thomas" version of the parable was produced by abridgement from the Synoptic Gospels.

[23] Ἀγαπητός is used in the LXX of Gen. xxii. 2, 12, 16, Jer. vi. 26, to translate yachid, of an only son (unless we suppose that in all these cases the translators read yadid for yachid), and there is other evidence that ἀγαπητός could bear that sense. See C. H. Turner in J. T. S., xxvii., pp. 113 sqq. The only child is as much a stock figure of folk-tale as the third son and the seventh.

[24] The Bezan and Koridethi texts, with some further support, have the Marcan order; but this is probably a case of assimilation.

is an introduction, the sequence of events is more clearly marked, and probably more true to fact, than we can assume it to be elsewhere), then the situation was one in which the veiled allusions might well be caught by many of the hearers. Jesus had, in the Triumphal Entry and the Cleansing of the Temple, challenged the public of Jerusalem to recognize the more-than-prophetic character of His mission. The parable might be understood as enforcing that challenge: "O Jerusalem, Jerusalem, that killest the prophets . . ."—what will the next step be? This is not allegory. It is a legitimate use of parable to bring out the full meaning of a situation.

Taken in this way, the parable of the Wicked Husbandmen helps to illuminate those sayings of Jesus in which He foretells His own death and the disaster to fall upon the Jews. The parable in itself gives expression to a moral judgment upon the situation; but by implication it may be said to " predict " the death of Jesus, and the judgment to fall upon His slayers. As I have already suggested, it is in this sense that the predictions are to be understood. They do not proceed from mere clairvoyance. They are a dramatization in terms of history of the moral realities of the situation.

Thus, although it is only in the secondary comment in Matthew that there is any allusion to the Kingdom of God, yet this parable is a true " parable of the Kingdom," since it points to the final crisis in the dealings of God with His people.

In all the cases we have so far considered there is no difficulty in seeing that the parables had a contemporary reference, and this reference has been generally recognized in the exegetical tradition. I want now to suggest that many other parables originally had a similar reference but this reference has been more or less obscured in our Gospels through the influence of readily recognizable motives arising out of the changed situation after the death of Jesus. First, however, we must try to see how the standpoint of the Church changed, and then illustrate the effect of this change on the interpretation of parables.

The early Church, which preserved the tradition of the teaching of Jesus, long kept the vivid sense of living in a new age which is implied in His declaration, " The Kingdom of God has come upon you." Beginning with the apostolic preaching, as we can recover it fragmentarily from the Acts of the Apostles, through the epistles of Paul and the Epistle to the Hebrews, on to the Fourth Gospel, the testimony of the Church is unanimous, that it is living in the age of fulfilment.[25] God has acted decisively in history, and the world is a new world.

Nevertheless the situation of the Church was different from the situation in which Jesus taught. When the apostles first made their proclamation, within a few weeks of the death of their Master, they may still have had the sense of living within the crisis, as they had lived during His brief ministry, though at a more advanced stage in it. They confidently expected that the whole meaning of the crisis would reveal itself before all eyes in the shortest possible time. But as the months and years passed by, the sense of crisis faded. Not all the things of which the Lord had spoken had come to pass. The Jewish community had not collapsed, and the temple stood. For years things went on, outwardly, as they had always been. The Lord had died, and He had risen again, and by the eye of faith they saw Him " on the right hand of God "; but where was the promise of His coming on the clouds of heaven?

In course of time the better minds of the Church, under the guidance of such teachers as Paul and the author of the Fourth Gospel, arrived at an interpretation which did justice to the deeper meaning of the teaching of Jesus. But meanwhile those who took his words literally built up a new Christian eschatology on the lines of the Jewish apocalyptic tradition. It is that which we have in outline in the " Little Apocalypse " of Mk. xiii, elaborated in Matthew, and it is brought to its completion in the Revelation of John.[26] The assumption is

[25] This is admirably enforced in Hoskyns and Davey, *The Riddle of the New Testament*.
[26] In the second century this tendency ran out into the popular Millenarianism which the leading minds of the Church came to regard as eccentric or worse, especially as it came to be associated with Montanism. The accepted position in the Church at large was a compromise. It took over the new eschatology, leaving large liberty to interpret its symbolism, but no longer attempted to fix a time-limit,

that at a date in the future (which the Church continued to the end of the first century to hope would soon come) the interrupted eschatological process will be resumed. The great tribulation will fall upon the Church, Jerusalem and the temple will fall, and the Son of Man will come on the clouds to judgment. Meanwhile the Church had its life to live in this world, and it gradually worked out a way of life which became more and more independent of eschatological expectations.

The result of this development was that the original unity and continuity of the eschatological process was broken up. This is the profound and significant difference between the outlook of the sayings of Jesus and that of the formed tradition of His teaching as it entered into our written Gospels. The sayings were uttered in and for a brief period of intense crisis : the tradition was formed in a period of stable and growing corporate life, conceived as the interval between two crises, one past, the other yet to come.

In this position, the Church, looking for guidance in the teaching of the Lord, would naturally tend to re-apply and re-interpret His sayings according to the needs of the new situation; and that in two ways (i) they would tend to give a general and permanent application to sayings originally directed towards an immediate and particular situation[27]; and (ii) they would tend to give to sayings which were originally associated with the historical crisis of the past, an application to the expected crisis of the future.

---

on the principle enunciated in II Pet. iii. 8. But the main emphasis rested upon that which had been done for man's redemption in Christ (the " realized eschatology " of the Gospels), and upon His abiding presence in the Church, especially guaranteed in the sacrament of the Eucharist.

[27] As I have said above (p. 79), I do not agree with those critics who hold that it was no part of the intention of Jesus to give ethical instruction of general application; but I do agree with them so far, that what we may call sayings of the occasion have at times been given a more general application. A notable example is the call to " bear the cross." This surely was a word for a single occasion, but Luke (ix. 23) has, by the addition of the word " daily," made it into a rule for Christian living. I do not say that this is illegitimate. I only say that we have every reason to believe that Jesus had a very particular situation in view.

These two motives, which we may describe as " homiletic "
or " paraenetic,"[28] and " eschatological," respectively, can be
shown, by comparison of one Gospel with another, to have
been at work during the period in which the Gospels were
written, and it is reasonable to suppose that they worked
during the earlier period of oral tradition. Let us then
examine some parables for traces of the influence of these
motives.

We may find a convenient starting-point in a parable which
occurs in Mt. v. 25-26 and Luke xii. 57-59, and which we
may call the parable of the Defendant. The two evangelists
have evidently taken the parable from a common source.
The differences between the two versions are few, and merely
verbal. In its Matthæan form the passage reads as follows: —

" Come to terms with your opponent quickly, while you
are with him on the way, lest your opponent should hand
you over to the judge, and the judge to the constable, and
you should be thrown in prison. Truly I tell you, you will
never get out till you have paid the last farthing."

It is clear that this is one of the parables transmitted without any application; neither evangelist has explicitly supplied
one. The contexts however in which they have placed the
parables indicate how they intended it to be applied.

In Matthew it forms part of the Sermon on the Mount,
and more particularly that section of the Sermon (v. 17-48)
in which various precepts of the old Law are criticized and
either reinterpreted, supplemented or superseded. The precept
" Thou shalt not kill " is cited. This is shown to be inadequate.
The law of Christ equally forbids anger and contempt. On the
positive side, reconciliation with a " brother " must take precedence even of the worship of God. It is the phrase " be

[28] Recent German scholars use the term "Paränese," representing
the Greek παραίνεσις to denote the distinctive form in which ethical
precepts are conveyed in the Synoptic Gospels, the ethical sections of
the Pauline epistles, and other parts of the N.T. Παραινεῖν is to advise,
recommend or exhort, and " paraenesis " seems an apt word to describe
the type of teaching in question. " Moral instruction " suggests something at once more systematic and colder in tone than what we have.
" Exhortation " perhaps has a suggestion of the rhetorical; it is
παράκλησις rather than παραίνεσις.

reconciled with your brother" (v. 24), that forms the link introducing the parable. What if your "brother" is your opponent in a law-suit? Well, even common sense suggests that you should "come to terms with your opponent quickly." It is clear that Matthew understood the parable to teach the importance of being always ready and anxious to take the first step towards the healing of a quarrel between neighbours. It is in this sense that it finds a place in the Sermon on the Mount, which is in fact a compilation of religious and moral maxims, drawn from the teaching of Jesus, for the guidance of Christians.

In Luke the context is different. In the preceding passage we have first a series of parables which we must later consider in detail—the Waiting Servants, the Thief at Night, the Faithful and Unfaithful Servants—and then another little parable about the punishment of disobedient servants. Then comes the great saying, "I came to set fire to the earth," introducing a description of the break-up of families. All this circles about the central idea of a crisis which provides a decisive test of men's dispositions and determines their destiny. Then follows the saying about the signs of the weather, the purport of which, in this context, is clearly to suggest that men ought to have the wit to see that the crisis is upon them.[29] Then follows our parable.

In this context the emphasis clearly falls upon the situation in which the defendant finds himself. He is being arrested for debt; in a few moments he will find himself in court, and he will no longer be a free man: sentence and imprisonment will inevitably follow. For the moment he is free to act. What shall he do? Common sense dictates: settle the case out of court with all speed. It is another picture of crisis, bringing out the urgent necessity of immediate action. Luke has suggested the application of this idea to the situation to which the preceding verses have pointed in the words, "Why do you not form a right judgment from yourselves?"—that

[29] The parable of the Fig-tree as Herald of Summer (Mk. xiii. 28) has a similar purport. Although this and the saying about the signs of the weather are referred by the evangelists to signs of the second advent still in the future, they are both surely more pointed if Jesus was calling upon men to recognize the significance of the situation in which, at the moment, they stood.

is neither out of your own sense of which is fitting, or from
the example of the behaviour set forth in the parable, which
is that of any man of ordinary common sense. In any case
he understands the parable to refer to the urgency of taking
the right step in face of the tremendous crisis which he has
depicted.

If now we take the parable out of its context, as it was
handed down in tradition, we must surely judge that Luke
has come nearer than Matthew to its primary significance.
It is not upon reconciliation as such that the emphasis falls.
More telling illustrations of the importance of reconciliation
could be found than a case in which it is, after all, only a matter
of expediency. But it provides an admirable foil to the in-
credible folly of men who, faced by a tremendous crisis, have
not the wit to see that they must act, now or never. If now
we recall that the preaching of Jesus was focused upon the
point that " the Kingdom of God has come upon you," we
are surely safe in concluding that the parable as He spoke it
was meant to be applied by the hearers to the situation in
which, then and there, they stood, faced by the supreme crisis
of all history. This was the original application. Luke, naturally enough, applies the same lesson to Christians awaiting
the future crisis of the Lord's second advent, while in Matthew
the " parænetic " motive has brought the parable into a quite
fresh setting.

A more complicated example is the treatment by the several
evangelists of the little parable about Salt. This parable is
found in all three Synoptics, and as Matthew and Luke agree
in significant variations from the Marcan form, we may safely
conclude that they found it in a common source independent
of Mark. The Marcan version is the simplest:

" Salt is good; but if the salt becomes saltless, with what
will you season it?" (ix. 50).

A comparison of Matthew (v. 13) and Luke (xiv. 34-35)
suggests that their common source had a form of the parable
somewhat as follows:

" If salt decays, with what will it be salted? It is good
for nothing; they throw it away."

Both Matthew and Mark explicitly indicate the application
which they intend. Luke gives no explicit application, but
the context in which he has placed the parable suggests the
way in which he understood it.

The Matthæan application (v. 13) is the clearest : " You
are the salt of the earth." The parable then becomes a warning
to the followers of Christ. Upon them lies the solemn responsibility of exerting a purifying and preservative influence
in the world at large : if they fail to do so, they have missed
the end of life, and will be utterly rejected by God.

The Marcan application (ix. 50) is given in the words,
" Have salt in (or among) yourselves, and live at peace with
one another." The meaning is not altogether perspicuous;
but in any case " salt " is not the Christian community itself
but some quality which it should possess; and it is a quality
somehow associated with " peace." Hence the salt-parable
is employed to close a series of sayings introduced by a scene
in which the disciples quarrel about precedence.[30] Perhaps
we should find an allusion to the widespread idea of salt as
a symbol of hospitality, and so of the permanent relation of
friendship set up between two who have partaken of each
other's salt. This cannot be regarded as a very felicitous
application; for the main point of the parable is the worth-
lessness of salt that has lost its savour, and it is just this point
which is left vague in the application.

In Luke (xiv. 34-35) the salt-parable closes a series of
sayings dealing with the stringent demands made upon those
who would follow Jesus, and introducing the two parables
of the builder who was not able to finish, and the king going

[30] The series of sayings is somewhat miscellaneous, and the links
between them are sometimes slender, turning upon the repetition of a
keyword. Thus the sayings in 42 and 43-47 respectively seem to be
linked only by the recurrence of the verb σκανδαλίζειν. The reference
to πῦρ in 43 and 48 leads to the cryptic saying in 49, πᾶς γὰρ πυρὶ
ἁλισθήσεται, and the verb ἁλίζειν in turn to the saying about salt. But
it seems clear that in the words ἔχετε ἐν ἑαυτοῖς ἅλα καὶ εἰρηνεύετε ἐν
ἀλλήλοις we are brought back to the situation in 34.

to war against a stronger enemy. The lesson of these parables is summed up in the words, "Even so, everyone of you who does not renounce everything of his own cannot be my disciple." Then follows the parable: "Salt is good, but if ever the salt decays, with what will it be seasoned?" The savourless salt is made to suggest the would-be disciple who does not fulfil the demand for renunciation. It is not clear whether salt is thought of as representing a quality, lacking which a man is not fit to follow Jesus, or as representing the person himself. Perhaps the latter is the simpler. In that case the sense approximates to that of Mt. v. 13; but whereas in Matthew the salt-like quality is a matter of influence in the world, in Luke the astringent savour of salt stands for the heroic virtue of the true Christian.

The variety of application suggested by the three evangelists shows that the primitive tradition did not know how the parable was originally intended to be applied. The use made of it in Mark and in Luke has an appearance of artificiality, and we can hardly think that the salt-parable was originally intended to suggest either peace in the Church or self-sacrifice. Matthew's interpretation is clear and effective. But was this the original intention of the parable?

Let us take it in isolation from any context, as it appears to have stood in the primitive tradition. Here is a picture of a commodity valuable to men, and indeed necessary to their life; but it has lost the one and only property which gives it value. It is worse than useless. Now in the situation in which Jesus taught, what was the most outstanding example in His eyes, of such a tragic loss of value? There is abundant evidence that He saw in the state of Judaism in His time just such a tragedy. We need not ask whether the "salt" of the parable is the Jewish people itself, or their religion.[81] The *tertium comparationis* is simply the lamentable fact of a good and necessary thing irrevocably spoiled and wasted. Applied in this way, the parable falls into line with other sayings of Jesus. It becomes a poignant comment on the whole situation at the moment. The evangelists, having lost

[81] The Torah is compared to salt in a Talmudic passage cited by Strack-Billerbeck on Mt. v. 13.

the sense of the moment, have in various ways utilized the parable to convey a lesson or warning to the Church of their own day.

The case is somewhat similar with the striking little parable of the Lamp and the Bushel. Here again we have a passage contained both in Mark and in the common source of Matthew and Luke. The Marcan version runs:

"Does the lamp come in to be put under the meal-tub or under the bed? Does it not come in to be put on the lamp-stand?" (iv. 21).

The Matthæan (v. 15) version runs as follows:

"They do not light a lamp and put it under the meal-tub, but on the lampstand, and then it gives light to all in the house."

It is probable that the original "Q" form was closely similar to this.[32]

Matthew alone gives an explicit application of the parable, in the words: "In the same way let your light shine before men, in order that they may see your good works, and glorify your Father in heaven." We may observe that this is a somewhat surprising maxim in the mouth of Jesus, when we con-

[32] The two Lucan versions have variations which can be explained. In viii. 16, Luke is conflating Mark and "Q" and hence introduces the "bed." In xi. 33 he suggests the "cellar" as a possible hiding-place. In both places he says that the lamp is placed on the lampstand "in order that all who are entering may see the light." That is, he conceives the lamp as standing in the vestibule of a house of the Græco-Roman type, as such houses at Pompeii show a niche for a lamp in the vestibule. Matthew has in view a Galilæan "but-and-ben," where there is one living-room, so that a single lamp suffices for the whole family. No doubt the "cellar" is also a feature of the more pretentious house which Luke has in view, whereas in the cottage, if you want to hide a lamp, there is no place for it but under the meal-tub, or perhaps under the bed. The Matthæan οὐδε καίουσιν λύχνον, following the Aramaic impersonal third plural used for the passive, is more likely to be original than the Lucan οὐδεὶς ἅψας. In any case the "Q" version had a negative statement where Mark has a question.

sider His stern sayings about those who do their righteousness to be seen of men; and also that it is closely similar to current Rabbinic teaching.[33]

In the other two Gospels we are left to infer the application from the context in which the parable is placed. In Mark it comes in a passage which is introduced by a question of the disciples regarding the nature and purpose of parables (iv. 10). To this the answer is given that the truth about the Kingdom of God is proclaimed in parables in order that " outsiders " may not understand it. Next, by way of example, an interpretation of the parable of the Sower is offered. Then comes the parable of the Lamp and the Bushel, followed by the saying " Nothing is hidden, but with the intention that[34] it shall be made manifest." It seems clear therefore that Mark thought the lamp represented the truth concerning the Kingdom of God, which in the lifetime of Jesus was concealed, but only with the ultimate intention that it should be displayed to the world like a lamp on a lampstand. That this connection is artificial hardly requires proof.

In Lk. viii. 16 the context is that of Mark. In xi. 33 the parable has a different setting. Here we have a series of sayings introduced by the words " This generation is a wicked generation; it seeks a sign." The general theme is the idea of a self-evident truth which needs no sign to confirm it. The Ninevites discerned the truth in the preaching of Jonah; the Queen of the South recognized the wisdom of Solomon—for a lamp on a lampstand gives light to all who enter the house.[35] For this evangelist then the lamp represents truth shining by its own light. This is hardly original, for it suggests no very pointed application of the idea of putting a lamp under a meal-tub, which is surely the main point of the parable.

It is evident that in the primitive traditon the parable came down without any express application. Each evangelist did his

[33] As richly illustrated by Strack-Billerbeck, *ad loc.*

[34] This must be the meaning of Mark's ἐὰν μὴ ἵνα: probably the Aramaic particle *di* has been understood as a final conjunction, while the " Q " form of the saying results if it be taken as a relative pronoun. The particle has both meanings.

[35] In the next verse there is a certain shift of meaning: " the lamp of the body is the eye." The Lucan interpretation therefore is not entirely consistent.

best with it, but none of the suggested applications seems entirely satisfactory. Let us then once again consider the parable by itself. It draws a picture of the extreme folly of putting a lighted lamp in the very place where its light becomes useless. In the situation in which Jesus spoke, what was the outstanding example of such folly? Was it not, in His eyes, the conduct of the religious leaders of His time, who, as He said, shut the Kingdom of Heaven in men's faces (Mt. xxiii. 13, Lk. xi. 52), or in other words, hid from them the light of God's revelation?[36] Once again, therefore, we seem to have a parable which was originally a biting comment upon the actual situation, but which the evangelists have used to convey teaching or warning to the Church of their day: to wit, either that Christians should show forth God's glory by their good works; or that the time has come when the mystery of the Kingdom of God should be blazoned abroad; or in general that truth shines by its own light.

These examples suffice to prove that what I have called the " parænetic " motive has in some cases worked to modify the original application of parables. In the next example I shall take this motive is replaced or supplemented by the " eschatological " motive.

The parable of the Talents in Matthew (xxv. 14-30) and the parable of the Pounds in Luke (xix. 12-27) are clearly variant versions of the same parable. The extent indeed to which they use the same words is not sufficient to make it likely that both evangelists followed the same proximate source; and there are differences in the actual story which make it probable that in both cases the *pericopé* had a history in tradition before it reached the evangelists. Nevertheless it is in substance the same story.

In the First Gospel the parable is one of a series appended to the apocalyptic discourse which is taken from Mark. The discourse itself focused upon the point of the advent of the Son of Man in glory at a time which is left indefinite, but is conceived as relatively remote in the future, though it

[36] Note that the Torah is light. See Strack-Billerbeck on Jn. i. 1-4 (*Kommentar*, II, p. 357).

will fall within the lifetime of the existing generation. Matthew then appends sayings to illustrate the unexpectedness of the advent: the saying about Noah's Flood, the parables of the Thief at Night and of the Faithful and Unfaithful Servants. Next he gives the parable of the Ten Virgins, which in another way enforces the wisdom of preparedness for the great event. Then follows the parable of the Talents, which in this context is clearly intended to refer to the second advent, and to serve as a warning to the followers of Christ that at His coming He will take account of the way in which they have borne their special responsibilities.

Luke has provided a brief introduction to the parable, which indicates clearly the application which he intended:

> "He spoke a parable, because he was near to Jerusalem, and because they supposed that the Kingdom of God would appear immediately."

The effect of this is to draw special attention to that part of the story which speaks of the master as taking a long journey and then returning to take account. The parable is made explicitly to teach a letter concerning the delay of the second advent.

Apart however from the application indicated in Matthew by the context and in Luke by the short introduction, both versions of the parable append a "moral." The Lucan form is the simpler:

> "To him who has, shall be given, and from him who has not, even what he has shall be taken away."

The Matthæan form differs only slightly:

> "To everyone who has shall be given, and he shall have abundance, and he who has not, even that he has shall be taken from him."[37]

---

[37] The somewhat rougher grammar of Matthew is probably more original, but he has added the words παντὶ and καὶ περισσευθήσεται. The common original can easily be restored.

It appears that the early traditional source which lies behind both versions supplied the parable with an application in the form of a general maxim. At a stage much earlier than that represented by the First and Third Gospels the point of the parable was felt to lie, not in the reference to the second advent, or to its delay, but to the specific treatment of the worthy and unworthy servants.

But it is to be observed that the same maxim appears in Mk. iv. 25 as a detached saying. It differs from the Lucan form only in its grammatical structure,[38] which more clearly betrays the influence of an underlying Aramaic original.[39] In this context Luke has copied Mark, with negligible differences, while Matthew has again introduced his additional words.

Now when we recall that there was a tendency to turn sayings of Jesus, which were uttered in reference to a particular situation, into general maxims for the guidance of the Church, we can no longer feel sure that the " moral " appended in the early traditional source to the parable of the Talents is original. As Matthew found in the parable of the Defendant an exhortation to reconciliation, and as Luke found in the parable of the Lamp and the Bushel an illustration of the principle that truth shines by its own light, so at an early stage the parable of the Money in Trust was used to illustrate the maxim that a man who possesses spiritual capacity will enlarge that capacity by experience, while a man who has none will decline into a worse condition as time goes on. That the maxim is an original saying of Jesus is fairly certain, in view of its multiple attestation, but its original application is lost beyond recall. In any case, the parable of the Money in Trust is not a perfect illustration of the principle. The man who

---

[38] ''Ος γὰρ ἔχει δοθήσεται αὐτῷ, καὶ ὅς οὐκ ἔχει, καὶ ὃ ἔχει ἀρθήσεται ἀπ᾽ αὐτοῦ. The substitution of the participial construction for the relative clause in Mt. xxv. 29 and Lk. xix. 26 improves the Greek.

[39] Mark has placed the saying in the series of utterances following the disciples' question about the nature and purpose of parables. Apparently he interpreted it with reference to the spiritual insight needed for their understanding. He who possesses spiritual insight will have that insight enlarged by considering the parables; he who does not possess it will only be led by them into worse bewilderment and ignorance. A true observation, but perhaps not the original purport of the saying.

hid the money was deprived of it, not because he had little
but because he had not increased his holding, which is a
different matter.

We must therefore postulate a still earlier form of the
parable in which, like so many of the parables of Jesus, it had
no expressed moral or application. Let us therefore take the
story by itself and try to bring it into relation with the actual
situation in the life of Jesus. For our purpose we shall do
well to construct the story so far as possible and of those elements which are common to Matthew and Luke, neglecting the
elaborations which are peculiar to one or other evangelist.

A man called his servants and gave them sums of money
in trust, and went away. Later he returned and called them
to account. Two of them had largely increased their capital
and were commended. A third confessed that he had been
afraid to risk his master's money, and had carefully hoarded
it: he now restored the precise sum he had received. It is
implied that he expected to be commended for his caution
and strict honesty. The master however retorted (and here the
agreement between the two versions is at its maximum):
"Wicked slave! You knew me for a man to drive a hard
bargain. You ought to have invested my capital, and then I
should have got it back with interest." The third servant is
thereupon deprived of his money, which is given to his more
enterprising colleague. There the story ended, so far as we can
reconstruct the earlier version.

It is surely evident that the central interest lies in the scene
of the reckoning, and in particular in the position of the
cautious servant, whose hopeful complacency receives so rude
a rebuff. The details of the story are subordinate to this
dramatic climax. The master's journey is necessary in order
to provide an interval during which the servants can prove
their worth. It has no independent interest. All is contrived
to throw into strong relief the character of the scrupulous
servant who will take no risks. It is upon his conduct that
the judgment of the hearers of the parable is invited. Here
is a man who with money to use will not risk its loss by investment, but hoards it in a stocking. An over-cautious, unenter-
prising person, we judge, too careful and too fearful to make

his mark. But, further, the money belongs to someone else, and was entrusted to him for investment. His over-caution, then, takes a worse colour. It amounts to a breach of trust. He is an unprofitable servant, a barren rascal. That is the judgment which the parable is intended to elicit.

To whom, then, is the judgment to be applied? In seeking an answer to this question we must put ourselves in the position of those who heard Jesus speak, and who would find a clue to His meaning, if at all, in their own experience and within the field of their own knowledge. While we need seek for no correspondence in historical facts with the details of the story, we may recall that in the Old Testament and in Jewish usage the relation of God and Israel was so constantly represented as that of a " lord " and his " slaves " that a hearer of the parable would almost inevitably seek an interpretation along those lines. Then who is the servant of God who is condemned for an over-caution amounting to breach of trust? I would suggest that he is the type of pious Jew who comes in for so much criticism in the Gospels. He seeks personal security in a meticulous observance of the Law. He " builds a hedge about the Law," and tithes mint, anise and cummin, to win merit in the sight of God. " All these things," he says, " I have observed from my youth "—" Lo, there Thou hast what is Thine!" Meanwhile, by a policy of selfish exclusiveness, he makes the religion of Israel barren. Simple folk, publicans and sinners, Gentiles, have no benefit from the Pharisaic observance of the Law, and God has no interest on His capital.

The parable,[40] I suggest, was intended to lead such persons to see their conduct in its true light. They are not giving God His own; they are defrauding Him. " The Judaism of that time," says Dr. Klausner,[41] " had no other aim than to save the tiny nation, the guardian of great ideals, from sinking into the broad sea of heathen culture." Put that way, it seems a legitimate aim. But from another point of view, might it not be aptly described as hiding the treasure in a napkin? To abandon the scrupulous discipline of Pharisaism would be a risk, no doubt. It was precisely the risk that the early

[40] Cf. Cadoux, *op. cit.*, pp. 106 sqq.   [41] *Jesus of Nazareth*, p. 376.

Christians took, and they took it under the inspiration of their Master. It is the kind of risk, this parable suggests, that all investment of capital involves; but without the risk of investment the capital remains barren. We have here, it seems, a pointed application of the parable which arises directly out of the historical situation.

If this argument is sound, we can trace in the history of this particular *pericopé* of the Gospels three stages. First, the parable is told by Jesus, with pointed reference to the actual situation. Next the early Church makes use of the parable for paraenetic purposes, applying it as an illustration of the maxim, " To him that hath shall be given." It is at this stage that the form of the parable underlying Matthew and Luke was fixed in tradition. In the Matthæan line of tradition it suffered further " paraenetic " developments. The amounts of money given to the three servants are now graded, in order that the parable may illustrate the varieties of human endowments.[42]

At a third stage the " paraenetic " motive is superseded or supplemented by the " eschatological " interest. The return of the master signifies the second advent of Christ, and the parable is on the way to become an allegory. In Matthew the unprofitable servant is not only deprived of his unused money; he is cast into outer darkness, where there shall be weeping and gnashing of teeth. The master's reckoning with his servants has become the Last Judgment. In Luke the allegory is carried further, along different lines. The master becomes a nobleman who goes into a far country to receive a kingdom.[43] That is Christ, who ascends to heaven to return as King. After taking reckoning with his servants, the King slays his enemies. That again is Christ who returning as judge will destroy the wicked. To put the reference to the second advent beyond all doubt, the parable is now introduced by a statement that it was spoken because some people thought

[42] The Gospel according to the Hebrews again has a different " paraenetic " development.

[43] It has often been suggested that the story has been influenced by reminiscences of the relations of the Herodian princes, especially Archelaus, with Rome. But the intention is allegorical.

that the Kingdom of God should immediately appear (whereas, as the Church now knew, there would be a long delay before the Lord's second coming).

The study of this parable has revealed how subtly the changing interests of the Church have altered the application, while leaving the substance of the story unaltered. We may fairly suspect that the same thing has happened in other cases, where the course of development is perhaps not so clear.

Chapter V

PARABLES OF CRISIS

There is a striking group of parables which as we have them are intended to be referred directly to the expected second advent of Christ, and to inculcate preparedness for that approaching crisis. It is in these parables that support is most commonly sought and found for the view, which I believe to be mistaken, that Jesus foretold a period of waiting between His death and resurrection and His coming in glory. The group consists of the parables of the Faithful and Unfaithful Servants, the Waiting Servants, the Thief at Night, and the Ten Virgins.

These parables, as we have them, are set in the context of exhortations to be ready, alert, wide-awake. Such exhortations belong to the current *parænesis* of the early Church. In the earliest extant Christian writing (as I believe it to be), the First Epistle to the Thessalonians, we have the following passage :

" You yourselves know quite well that the Day of the Lord comes like a thief at night. When they are saying, ' Peace and security,' then suddenly destruction comes upon them like her pangs upon a woman with child, and they certainly will not escape. But you, brothers, are not in darkness, that the Day should overtake you like a thief. For you are all sons of light and sons of day. We do not belong to night or darkness. Let us therefore not sleep as others do, but let us keep awake and be sober. For sleepers sleep by night and drunkards are drunk by night; but let us who belong to day be sober " (v. 2-8).

As Paul says that this is familiar to his readers, we may take it that such exhortations were a regular part of the instruction he was accustomed to give to his converts. Now compare the following passage, which Luke has added to the apocalyptic discourse taken from Mark:

> "Beware lest your hearts be made heavy with revelling and drunkenness and worldly cares, and that Day come upon you like a snare. For it will come upon all who dwell on the face of the whole earth. But keep awake,[1] praying on every occasion for strength to escape all these things which are going to happen, and to stand before the Son of Man" (xxi. 34-36).

The general similarity of the two passages is striking, and the similarity extends to the actual language.[2] That Paul is quoting from the Gospel is impossible. That the evangelist had heard Paul give such teaching is possible.[3] The probability is that both passages represent a common type of early Christian preaching at least in missions to the Gentiles.

Similar language recurs in other Pauline epistles, notably in Eph. v. 8-14:

> "You were once darkness, but now are light in the Lord. Conduct yourselves as children of light . . . and have no association with the barren deeds of darkness. . . .Wherefore it says.
>
> ' Awake thou that sleepest,

[1] It seems necessary to call attention to an ambiguity of our language. The English word " watch " is etymologically identical with " wake," and formerly bore the same meaning. But in common usage at the present time to " watch " is to observe, to look out for, to be on guard, or the like: it corresponds to such Greek words as θεωρεῖν, παρατηρεῖσθαι, φυλάττειν. But these are not the words used in the passages referred to; they are γρηγορεῖν and ἀγρυπνεῖν, and these mean " to keep awake," with the implication of alertness—that and nothing else. The change in meaning in the English word " watch " makes it a most misleading translation.

[2] In I Thess., αιφνίδιος . . . ἐπίσταται . . . οὐ μὴ ἐκφύγωσιν . . . η ἡμέρα . . . γρηγορῶμεν . . . μεθύσκόμενοι . . . μεθύουσιν. In Lk., μέθη . . . ἐπιστῇ ἐφ' ὑμᾶς αιφνίδιος η ἡμέρα ἐκείνη . . . ἀγρυπνεῖτε 'λιϑλαφχϑ · · ·

[3] If the author of the third Gospel was Luke, Paul's medical attendant, then we know that he had been with Paul during part at least of the journey which included the visit to Thessalonica (Acts xvi. 11-13, xvii. 1).

> And arise from the dead,
> And Christ will shine upon thee.' "

The citation of what must be an early Christian hymn shows that we are here dealing not with the teaching of an individual but with ideas current in the early Church. The Christian is one who is fully awake; the life of sin is a sleep. We are reminded of moral exhortations in non-Christian religious works of similar date. Thus in the Hermetic tractate called *Poimandres* we read:

> " O peoples, earthborn men, who have given yourselves over to drunkenness and sleep and ignorance of God, cease revelling under the enchantment of irrational sleep. . . Depart from the light which is darkness."[4]

The exhortation therefore to " awake out of sleep " seems to have been something like a commonplace of moralists at the time. The peculiarity of the type of teaching represented by the passages quoted from I Thessalonians and the Third Gospel is the introduction of the eschatological motive.[5] The

---

[4] *Corpus Hermeticum*, I, 27. Note the words μέθη καὶ ὕπνῳ, κραιπαλῶντες, τοῦ σκοτεινοῦ φωτός, which recall the association of sleep and drunkenness in I Thess. v., Lk. xxi. (as well as Rom. xiii. 11-13), the use of κραιπάλη in Lk. xxi., and the contrast of light and darkness in I Thess. v. and Rom. xiii. Cf. also *Corp. Herm.*, VII, 1-2, and see my book, *The Bible and the Greeks*, pp. 183-186. Similarly, in the *Testaments of the Twelve Patriarchs* the " spirit of sleep " is a spirit of πλάνη and φαντασία and is associated (συνάπτεται) with the " spirits " of falsehood, arrogance, injustice, fornication and the like (*Test. Reub.*, iii. 1-7: Charles suspects interpolation after the Testaments were translated into Greek; but for our purpose this is unimportant).

[5] Observe the subtle way in which Paul passes from the idea of the " Day of the Lord " to the idea of " day " as opposed to " night," *i.e.* " light " as opposed to " darkness," in the sense of teaching like that of the *Hermetica*. In the passage from Ephesians the standpoint is that which is common to Christianity and to Hellenistic teaching, except that the idea of " resurrection " takes the place of the idea of the attainment of " immortality." That is characteristic. That the Christian is " risen from the dead " follows from the " realized eschatology " of the Gospels. The Kingdom of God has come; the " Age to Come " has come; the " life of the Age to Come " is realized.

reason for "wakefulness" is the certain approach, and the uncertain date, of the second advent of Christ. Whether or not this kind of teaching was directly derived from the teaching of Jesus, it was current in the Church. It is given by Paul in his own person, and placed by Luke in the mouth of Jesus. That being so, it is only what we should expect that any of His parables which seemed to lend themselves to the purpose would be applied in this sense. The example of the parable of the Money in Trust, which we have just considered, will warn us that such an application is not *necessarily* the one originally intended.

With this preface we may turn to the parables with which we are immediately concerned.

We may start with the parable of the Faithful and Unfaithful Servants. It is given by Matthew (xxiv. 45-51) and by Luke (xii. 42-46) with such striking identity of language, and with such insignificant variations, that there is no difficulty in recognizing the original " Q " form of the *pericopé*. In that form it has no explicit application. The context alone makes clear the sense that the evangelists attached to it. The parable, like several others, opens with a question—an opening which betrays the essential purpose of a parable, to elicit a judgment from the hearers.

" Who is the faithful, prudent slave,[6] whom his master set[7] over his household, to give them their food at the proper time? Blessed is that slave whom his master on his arrival will find so doing. Truly I tell you, he will set him over his entire property. But if the wicked slave says in his heart, ' My master is delaying his arrival,' and begins to beat his fellow-slaves, and to eat and drink with the drunken, the master of that slave will come on a day when he does not expect him, and at a moment he does not know, and he

[6] Δοῦλος in Matthew, οικονόμος in Luke: but elsewhere δοῦλος in both. The function of the slave is that of an οικονόμος.

[7] Κατέστησεν, Matthew; καταστήσει, Luke. Elsewhere in both the verbs are future, but it is appropriate that the verb which expresses the situation out of which the whole story develops should be in the past tense.

will cut him in two,[8] and appoint his lot with the unfaithful."[9]

In the story, the journey and return of the master receive
no emphasis. It is clearly no more than a necessary part of the
dramatic machinery, designed to produce the situation desired.
The emphasis lies upon the contrasting behaviour of two
persons placed in the like position. The one faithfully per-
forms the duty assigned to him; the other betrays his trust by
self-indulgence. That in both cases the responsibility must
be borne in the absence of the master is clearly essential. Now
we ask, What would such a picture be expected to suggest to
hearers of Jesus who knew nothing of a long delay of His
second advent? They were familiar with the idea of Israel
as the servant of the Lord[10], and in particular of outstanding
figures in the history of Israel, such as leaders, rulers and
prophets, as in an especial sense His servants.[11] Surely they
would think of persons who at that time stood in an analogous
position: the chief priests and scribes who " sat in Moses's[12]
seat " (Mt. xxiii. 2.) The parable therefore appears to pillory
the religious leaders of the Jews as God's unfaithful servants,

---

[8] Διχοτομήσει. This barbarous punishment was sufficiently well
known. But it is difficult to see how a " dichotomized " person could
afterwards be given his portion with the unfaithful. No doubt it would
be possible to understand the meaning to be, " he will cut him in two,
thereby appointing his lot with the unfaithful "; but this is strained.
Two explanations are possible: (i) the last clause is an allegorizing
supplement; the lot of the ἄπιστοι (" unbelievers ") is to be destroyed;
this is what the cutting in two really signifies; (ii) we may have a case
of mistranslation : the original Aramaic may have meant simply
" will cut him off," i.e. will expel him from the household, or it may
have read "will divide him his portion with the unfaithful," a good
Aramaic idiom (so Torrey, The Four Gospels, ad loc.).

[9] Ἀπίστων, Luke; ὑποκριτῶν, Matthew. The latter word is characteristic of the First Gospel. If this word is read, then the clause is
clearly and allegorizing supplement, for the ὑποκριταί are no characters in the story. But ἀπίστων is certainly original : the whole parable
turns on the contrast πιστός/ἄπιστος.

[10] See The Bible and the Greeks, pp. 9-11. Cf. Ps. cxxxvi. 22;
Is. xli. 8, etc.

[11] Abraham, Moses, David, Hezekiah, Zerubbabel, the prophets
Ahijah, Isaiah, and Jonah, and others, are so described. Hebrew,
'ebed; Greek, δοῦλος or παῖς.

[12] " My servant Moses " is a standing title, and Moses is emphatically
the " faithful " servant of Jehovah, Num. xii. 7.

exactly as in another parable they are pilloried as Wicked Husbandmen, and as the unprofitable servant in the parable of the Money in Trust. It had a sharp point directed to the actual situation. When that situation had passed, the Church, naturally enough, and legitimately enough, re-applied it to their own different situation.

The parables of the Waiting Servants in Mark and in Luke respectively present a complicated problem. The passage in Lk. xii. 35-38 runs as follows:

"Have your loins girt and your lamps burning, and be like men awaiting their master's return from the wedding, in order that when he arrives and knocks they may open to him at once. Blessed are those servants whom their master on his arrival will find awake. Truly I tell you he will gird himself, and make them sit down and come and wait upon them.[13] Even if he comes in the second or even in the third watch, and finds them so, blessed are they."

The corresponding passage in Mk. xiii. 33-37, runs as follows:

"Take heed: keep awake, for you do not know when the time is; like a man who left his house and went on a journey, and gave authority to his servants, assigning to each his task, and enjoined upon the porter to keep awake. Keep awake then, for you do not know when the master of the house is coming, late in the evening, or at midnight, or at cockcrow, or at dawn: lest he should come and find you asleep. And what I say to you, I say to all: keep awake."

Different though the two passages are, they have a common basis—the picture of the servants in a large household waiting for their absent master, who may return at any hour of the

[13] The use of διακονεῖν here, which is peculiar to Luke, recalls ἐγὼ δ᾿... ἀ᾿ μ᾿᾿ ὁ διακονῶν, (Lk. xxii. 27). It may have been suggested by that saying, which is given also in Mk. x. 45, in a somewhat different form, but preserving the verb διακονεῖν. In that case it is an allegorizing trait.

night. The fact that the divisions of the night are in Mark enumerated on the Roman reckoning and in Luke on the Jewish reckoning does not weaken the inference that the two versions represent a single original parable. We might infer that Luke preserves the more original reckoning, and that Mark has transposed it for his Roman audience; but the Roman reckoning was well-known in Palestine also. Further, in both cases the primary duty of the servants is to keep awake—to sit up for the master, in a common phrase.

This nucleus is variously expanded in the two Gospels. In Luke the master has gone to a wedding. This recalls the situation in the Matthæan parable of the Ten Virgins, though here it is not said the master is himself the bridegroom. Again, the commendation of the good servants is forcibly expressed in the repeated ' blessed,' which recalls the language of the parable of the Faithful and Unfaithful Servants, and may perhaps have been influenced by it.

The parable is applied in the words, " *Be like* men awaiting their master "; and it is amplified in the introductory sentence : " Let your loins be girt and your lamps burning." The latter is, as regards its first clause, a commonplace of moral exhortation.[14] while its second clause once again recalls the Matthæan parable of the Ten Virgins; there is nothing about lamps in the parable itself, though indeed no one could be expected to sit up all night without a light. It is clear enough that Luke, or his immediate authority, has understood the parable in the sense of an injunction to the followers of Christ to be alert for His second advent; and that he takes the successive watches of the night to suggest the long delay of that advent, which was causing distress and searching of heart in the Church. The introductory exhortation we may safely take to be a piece of homiletic matter, not originally part of the parable. The Clause " Be like men awaiting their master " may well have been the original introduction to the parable. If it was, the further question would remain : who are the persons addressed? For the evangelist of course, the waiting

[14] Cf. I Pet. i. 13. The expression is taken from the O.T., cf. Job xxxviii. 3, xl. 7; Jer. i. 17. (" Pull yourself together " is our colloquial equivalent.)

Church: but we do not know who the original audience may have been, whether the disciples of Jesus or the general public.

In Mark the details of the story are worked out differently. The opening, " like a man who went on a journey and gave authority to his servants," sounds like a reminiscence of the opening of the parable of the Money in Trust in its Matthæan form; " As a man who was going on a journey called his own servants and gave over to them his property." Whereas in Luke the servants in a body are expected to sit up for the master, to answer his knock, in Mark they have their several duties, and the task of the porter alone is to keep awake ready to open the door. These elaborations are still well within the framework of the fictitious situation. But thereupon the scene changes: the characters of the story melt into the figures of Christ and His followers: " Keep awake then, for *you* do not know when the Master of the House is coming . . . lest when He come He should find *you* asleep." In this setting it is made quite clear that the divisions of the night are a symbol for the lapse of time before the second advent. The application of the parable is enforced in similar terms in the introduction: " take heed: keep awake, for you do not know when the time is "; and this maxim is explicitly generalized for the benefit of Christians of a later day in the concluding phrase of the *pericopé*: " what I say to you, I say to all: keep awake."[15]

The parable therefore has become disintegrated by the effort to fix upon it beyond all question one particular interpretation. It is indeed the interpretation implied in Luke, but the process of re-interpretation under the influence of the " eschatological " motive has reached a more advanced stage.[16]

In Matthew all that remains of the *pericopé* is the injunction which in Mark points the moral of the parable, the story having disappeared; and that injunction is given

[15] The relation of this to Lk. xii. 41, where the reference is to the parable of the Thief at Night, and the words are used to introduce the parable of the Faithful and Unfaithful Servants, is puzzling, but for our purpose it is not important, except as indicating a definite tendency to generalize the application of these parables.

[16] We must therefore say, with Bacon, that the Lucan source here belongs to an earlier stratum than Mark.

with a significant change. Where Mark has "keep awake, for you do not know when the *master of the house* is coming," Matthew has (xxiv. 42): "Keep awake, because you do not know when *your Master* is coming." The parabolic character of the saying has disappeared.

It is clear that in the transmission of this *pericopé* the "eschatological" motive has been at work with especial force. The parable of the Waiting Servants seemed to the Church to depict more vividly than any other its own situation, as it anxiously awaited the consummation of its hopes—hopes deferred from evening to midnight, from midnight to cock-crow—while it heartened itself with the thought: "the night is far spent; the day is at hand" (Rom. xiii. 12).

But did Jesus Himself teach His disciples to anticipate His second advent after a long and incalculable interval? Was this parable intended to teach it?

Let us go back to the common nucleus of the parable as we recovered it from a comparison of Mark and Luke, bearing in mind that a parable is normally the dramatic presentation of a situation, intended to suggest vividly some single idea. Here the idea is that of alertness and preparedness for any emergency. It is felicitously suggested by the tense atmosphere of a great household when the master is away but may turn up at any hour of the night. All the vivid detail need serve no other purpose than that of creating the atmosphere.

We may then ask. What was the emergency which Jesus had in view? We know that He saw in His own ministry the supreme crisis in history. There is nothing in the parable itself against the view that the emergency He contemplated was in fact the crisis created by His own coming, rather than an expected crisis in the more or less distant future. The crisis which He brought about was not a single momentary event but a developing situation. If He said to the general public, "Be like men awaiting their master," he may have meant "Be alert and prepared for any development in this critical situation." If He addressed His own disciples, then we may compare the words which He spoke to them in Gethsemane: "Watch and pray, that ye enter not into temptation" (Mk. xiv. 38)[17]—the "temptation," or more properly, "testing-time,"

[17] Martin Dibelius, in an article in *The Crozer Quarterly*, July, 1935,

being in that case the immediately impending attack upon Him and His followers. Some such realistic reference to the immediate situation is most probably the clue to the meaning of the parable. It was not spoken to prepare the disciples for a long though indefinite period of waiting for the second advent, but to enforce the necessity for alertness in a crisis now upon them.

The parable of the Thief at Night in both Matthew (xxiv. 43-44) and Luke (xii. 39-40) immediately precedes that of the Faithful and Unfaithful Servants. The identity of order, together with the close similarity of the language in both Gospels, shows that it is taken from a common source. The original " Q " form can be easily recovered:

"You know that if the householder had known at what

---

pp. 254 sqq., discusses the Gethsemane narrative, and concludes that, so far at least as the words attributed to Jesus are concerned, it reflects the thought of the Church rather than any historical reminiscence. "'Watch and pray, that ye enter not into temptation.' From (sic.: read 'of' = 'von') this word it may be asserted that it is not spoken or conceived for this context. For if the temptation were meant which now, in the night of the passion, comes to the disciples, the warning to stay awake would be of no avail; even wide-awake disciples would be ensnared in this temptation. On the contrary, obviously the great eschatological temptation is meant . . . the call to watchfulness signifies what many N.T. passages seek to say with the same warning (cf. Mk. xiii. 35; I Cor. xvi. 13; I Pet. v. 8); the Lord is coming, but ye do not know when, therefore watch." Dibelius therefore recognizes the affinity of Mk. xiii. 35 with the utterance in Gethsemane; but I should interpret the evidence differently. The πειρασμός of Mk. xiv. 38 is, of course, as he says, the eschatological tribulation; but as Jesus declared that the Kingdom of God had come, all the events of His ministry and its immediate sequel are " eschatological " events, and I conceive Him to have recognized in the attack made upon Him and His disciples the approach of the great tribulation.

I do not contend that we have a verbatim report of what Jesus said, here, or indeed anywhere else (except possibly where His utterances were in the form of verse, which protected them from serious altera-tion, in the Aramaic original). But I do contend that the exhortation to be alert against the immediately impending " temptation " is appropri-ate to the situation in Gethsemane, and that the parable of the Waiting Servants, in its original form, was appropriate to a situation, shortly before this, when the attack was expected by Jesus, but the disciples were not aware of it.

hour[18] the thief would come, he[19] would not have allowed his house to be broken into."

The application follows immediately, in a form verbally identical in Matthew and Luke, and therefore belonging to the common source:

"Be you also ready, because the Son of Man is coming at a moment when you do not think (He is coming)."

The parable therefore was applied to the advent-expectation at the earliest stage of the tradition to which Gospel criticism can go back.

Not only so, but the Synoptic tradition is confirmed by the very early evidence of I Thessalonians:

"You know quite well that the Day of the Lord is coming like a thief at night" (v. 2).

This implies surely that Paul and his converts knew a tradition which contained the parable with an application substantially identical with that of "Q," except that Paul substitutes "the Day of the Lord" for "the Son of Man." This carries back the attestation to as early a stage in the history of the Church as it is possible to reach. We must of course reckon with the possibility that even at this very early stage the "eschatological" motive had been at work, for the growth of interest in the expectation of the second advent must have begun as soon as even a few years had elapsed since the Resurrection without bringing the expected consummation. In that case the parable might originally have referred to a signal example of unpreparedness for the unexpected in contemporary history. Such an interpretation might find some support in the form which the parable has taken in "Q"—a conditional sentence referring to the past, in which the condition is unfulfilled. If the householder *had* known, he *would not* have allowed his

[18] Ποίᾳ ὥρᾳ. Matthew has ποίᾳ φυλακῇ, a reminiscence of the parable of the Waiting Servants, which he has omitted.
[19] Matthew adds "would have been awake and"—another reminiscence of the parable of the Waiting Servants.

house to be broken into. This might suggest that someone had actually been taken by surprise. We might then compare the lament over Jerusalem in Luke: " If thou hadst but known, even thou in this thy day, the things that make for thy peace! . . . thou didst not recognize the day of thy visitation." The Kingdom of God has come—unexpectedly, incalculably— and Israel was taken by surprise.

We should however probably be wise to be guided by the extremely early tradition which found in the parable a warning to be ready for something which has not yet happened. This " something " is for Paul "the Day of the Lord " (in old prophetic language); for " Q " the coming of the Son of Man. In that case the nearest parallel is the saying about the Deluge, which is found in Matthew and Luke with comparatively slight variations. The simpler version is the Lucan, and this is probably very near to the original " Q " form:

" As it happened in the days of Noah, so shall it be in the days of the Son of Man.[20] They were eating, drinking, marrying and being married until the day when Noah entered the ark, and the deluge came and destroyed them all " (Lk. xvii. 26-27).

There is the same suggestion of complete unpreparedness for a sudden disaster.

Now I have suggested that the predictions of the coming of the Son of Man or of " that Day," in terms of a transcendent or supernatural order, are to be regarded as running parallel, in part at least, with the predictions of historical disaster. The coming of the Son of Man, in its aspect as judgment, is realized in the catastrophes which Jesus predicted as lying immediately in store—the persecution of Himself and His disciples, the destruction of the Temple and of the Jewish nation. These catastrophes He regarded as an immediately imminent development of the existing situation. Thus the care-free people eating and drinking at ease like the ante-

[20] Matthew has " so shall be the *parusia* of the Son of Man." The term *parusia* is used by Matthew alone among the Synoptics, and is no doubt intruded here. Did the original " Q " version give " the Day of the Son of Man," which would be equivalent to Paul's " Day of the Lord "?

diluvians are the men and women whom Jesus saw about Him, stupidly unaware that the judgments of God were in the earth, and destined at any moment to be overwhelmed with disaster. The disaster began: the authorities made their attack upon Jesus and His disciples. The disciples, although warned to watch and pray lest they enter into temptation, were after all unprepared, and were swept off their feet. If they had been alert, they would not have collapsed, just as if the householder had known beforehand of the intended burglary, he would have forestalled it.

So understood, this parable falls well into line with the parable of the Waiting Servants, as I have interpreted it.[21] Both were originally intended to refer to a situation already existing, but subject to unexpected developments at any moment. They were both intended to warn the hearers to be prepared for such developments. When the immediate crisis passed, the parables were naturally reapplied to the situation in which the early Christians found themselves after the death of Jesus; and as the expectation of the second advent hardened into a dogma, the details of the parable of the Waiting Servants lent themselves to re-interpretation in the sense of that dogma, while the brief parable of the Thief at Night passed into a simple simile for the suddenness of the expected event, as we find it in Paul.

In these three "eschatological" parables, then, we seem to have reflected a situation in the ministry of Jesus when the crisis He had provoked was hastening towards uncertain and unexpected developments, which called for the utmost alertness on the part of His followers. The same situation is reflected in the narrative of Mark from the scene at Cæsarea Philippi to Gethsemane; from the warning of imminent disaster which followed Peter's confession, to the urgent "Watch and pray," and the last word of all to the disciples, "The moment has arrived: the Son of Man is betrayed." Jesus is all through concerned to prepare His followers for the

[21] One is tempted to suggest that in the earliest tradition of all the Thief at Night and the Waiting Servants formed a pair, instead of the Waiting Servants and the Faithful and Unfaithful Servants, as in " Q." The existence of pairs of parables is a constant feature of the tradition, but the members of the pairs are sometimes different in different sources. See p. 154.

time of stress. The parables, rightly understood, take their place in that series of warnings and appeals.

In the light afforded by the study of these three short parables we may approach the more elaborate parable of the Ten Virgins in Mt. xxv. 1-12, which is placed between the parable of the Faithful and Unfaithful Servants and that of the Talents. It is introduced as a parable of the Kingdom : " Then the Kingdom of Heaven will be likened to ten virgins." At the close Matthew has appended, as a moral of the story, the now familiar maxim, " Keep awake therefore, because you know neither the day nor the hour." It is clear that for the evangelist the parable is a warning to be prepared for the future advent of the Son of Man, and this is for him the coming of the Kingdom of God. The story itself however is readily applicable to the situation in the ministry of Jesus, along the lines suggested by our study of the three companion parables. The moment of crisis is here represented by the appearance of the bridegroom and this is parallel with the return of the master in the parables of the Waiting Servants and of the Faithful and Unfaithful Servants. All the vivid dramatic detail is intended only to emphasize the folly of unpreparedness and the wisdom of preparedness—preparedness, as I take it, for the developments actually in process in the ministry of Jesus.

It is interesting to observe that, although this parable is peculiar to Matthew, yet certain elements in it seem to have intruded into the Lucan rendering of the Waiting Servants, viz, the lit lamps and the wedding. It looks, therefore, as though Luke had been acquainted with some form of the parable. It is particularly significant that the closing words of the parable are used by Luke, with slight verbal differences, in a different context. Says Matthew :

" The bridegroom came, and those who were ready went with him to the wedding. Afterwards the other maidens came, saying, ' Sir, open to us.' But he answered and said, ' Truly I tell you, I do not know you.' "

Now compare this with Luke xiii. 25 sqq. :

"From the time when the householder has got up and shut the door, you will begin to stand outside and knock at the door, saying, 'Lord, open to us.' And He will answer and say to you: 'I do not know where you come from.'"

It is surely clear that the source of the two passages is the same; but whereas in Matthew we have the natural conclusion of a quite realistic story, in Luke the only remnant of parable is in the word "householder." For the rest, the *dramatis personæ* have retired behind the figure of Christ as Judge, with His unrepentant hearers arraigned before Him.[22] Luke, in fact, has dealt with the parable of the Closed Door as Mark dealt with the parable of the Waiting Servants. The eschatological motive has disintegrated the parable and replaced it by direct prediction. This becomes even clearer as we read on:

"Then you will begin to say 'We ate and drank in thy presence, and thou didst teach in our streets.' And He will say, 'I do not know where you come from: depart from me, all workers of iniquity.'"

This belongs to the same general body of teaching as Mt. vii. 22-23:

"Many will say to *me* in that day: 'Lord, Lord, did we not prophesy in thy name, and in thy name cast out demons, and in thy name do many works of power?' And then I will profess to them. 'I never knew you: depart from me, you who commit lawlessness.'"

Here the final step has been taken. The "bridegroom" of Mt. xxv., the "householder" of Luke xiii., has become unequivocally the Lord Jesus speaking in His own person, and the scene is expressly laid on "that day"—the Day of Judgment to come.

It seems possible, therefore, to give to all these "eschato-

[22] That is why the word κύρις in Matthew has to be rendered by "Sir," as the customary mode of respectful address, and in Luke by "Lord."

logical " parables an application within the context of the ministry of Jesus. They were intended to enforce His appeal to men to recognise that the Kingdom of God was present in all its momentous consequences, and that by their conduct in the presence of this tremendous crisis they would judge themselves as faithful or unfaithful, wise or foolish. When the crisis had passed, they were adapted by the Church to enforce its appeal to men to prepare for the second and final world-crisis which it believed to be approaching.

Chapter VI

PARABLES OF GROWTH

There is a further group of parables distinguished by the fact that the idea of growth is common to them all: those of the Sower, the Tares, the Seed Growing Secretly and the Mustard Seed. With these we must consider the parables of the Leaven and of the Drag-net, which are closely connected in the Gospels with those of the Mustard Seed and the Tares respectively. Three of these parables are provided with an application in the formula " The Kingdom of God is like . . ." The parables of the Sower, the Tares, and the Drag-net are provided with allegorical "interpretations" which cannot be regarded as original.

The predominant interpretation of these parables makes them refer to the future history of the Kingdom of God in the world. If Jesus declared that the Kingdom of God had arrived, these parables indicate that it was present only in germ, and allow for an indefinite period of development before the consummation. The School of *consequente Eschatologie* modifies this only in the sense of a shortening of the period, pointing out that mustard is a quick-growing plant, or suggesting that the stages of sowing, growth and harvest were intended to correspond, literally, with the actual lapse of time between the beginning of the ministry of Jesus and the date at which He expected the catastrophic irruption of the Kingdom of God.[1] At no point does the eschatological interpretation of the Gospels appear more strained and artificial; and yet the alternative would seem to be to admit what we have hitherto ruled out—a lapse of time before the second advent.

We may begin with the parable of the Seed Growing Secretly in Mk. iv. 26-29:

[1] See Schweitzer, *Geschichte der Leben-Jesu-Forschung*, 1913, p. 403.

"The Kingdom of God is like this: as if a man should cast seed on the ground, and go to sleep and wake night and day; and the seed germinates and grows, he knows not how. Spontaneously the earth bears fruit—first blade, then ear, then full corn in the ear. But when the crop yields, at once he applies the sickle, because the harvest has come."

The application of the parable is simple and direct: the Kingdom of God is like this. It is true that we are still uncertain whether the Kingdom of God is like the seed, or like what happens when seed is sown: whether it is like the growth or like the harvest. There is therefore a difficult problem of interpretation.

Broadly speaking, modern interpretation has followed one of three lines:

(1) The Kingdom of God is like the seed: it is an inward germinal principle: "the Kingdom of God is within you." Either it is a divine principle within the soul, which develops until the whole character is transformed; or it is a divine principle at work in society, developing until society at large is comfortable to the divine will. In this case Jesus is conceived as the sower of the seed. He introduced into the world a creative principle, which works through the centuries to its fulfilment. This interpretation can appeal to the Matthæan interpretation of the parable of the Tares: "he who sows the good seed is the Son of Man."

(ii) The Kingdom of God is like the whole process of growth. It is the divine energy immanent in the world by which the purpose of God is gradually achieved. This interpretation can appeal to the word αὐτομάτη ("spontaneously"), and to the enumeration of the stages of growth. It was peculiarly sympathetic to the evolutionary thought of the nineteenth century, and was welcomed as giving a place to the conception of evolution within the teaching of Jesus Himself. The Harvest could then be thought of as that

"far-off divine event
To which the whole creation moves."[2]

[2] Unless indeed the concluding verse, which shows the influence of

It has the weakness of allowing no special place to the work of Jesus Himself. He neither sows the seed nor reaps the harvest, but declares the truth that the Kingdom of God comes of itself.

(iii) The Kingdom of God is like the harvest, and the rest of the story is subordinate to this. This is the interpretation favoured by the "eschatological" school. The view of the ministry of Jesus taken by this school is that it was altogether directed by the idea that the Kingdom of God would come very soon, by a catastrophic divine intervention. The sowing is, according to Dr. Schweitzer, "the movement of repentance awakened by John the Baptist and carried further by the preaching of Jesus"[3]; and He Himself will be the Harvester when, very shortly, the Kingdom of God comes and He is revealed in glory. The weakness of this interpretation is that it can make little of the stages of growth to which attention is drawn in the story itself.

Thus the interpretation of the parables depends upon the view taken of the Kingdom of God. The view taken in this book is that in the few explicit (not parabolic) statements which Jesus made about the coming of the Kingdom, it is neither an evolutionary process nor yet a catastrophic event in the near future, but a present crisis. It is not that the Kingdom of God will shortly come, but that it is a present fact; and not a present fact in the sense that it is a tendency towards righteousness always present in the world, but in the sense that something has now happened which never happened before.

Let us then consider the parable in the light of this. The harvest was an old and familiar symbol for the eschatological event, the Day of the Lord, the Day of Judgment. If the reference to harvest is original in the parable, this is undoubtedly the idea which it would suggest to the hearers, even without the specific allusion to a particular prophetic passage (Joel iii. 13). Now there is at least one allusion

Joel, should be put to the credit of the eschatological interest of the early Church (as Wellhausen); in that case the application of the parable is completely general.

[3] *Leben-Jesu-Forschung*, p. 403.

to harvest in the sayings of Jesus which has unmistakable reference not to the future, but to the existing situation (Mt. ix. 37-38=Lk. x. 2):

"The harvest truly is plentiful, but the labourers are few: pray therefore the Lord of the harvest to send labourers into His harvest."

A comparison of Matthew and Luke shows that in their common source this saying was the immediate preface to the "Mission-charge" delivered to the Twelve. According to "Q", therefore, when Jesus spoke of the harvest and the labourers he did not mean that "the reapers are the angels" (Mt. xiii. 39). He was there and then sending out His disciples as labourers to reap the harvest which was already ripe for in-gathering.

It is natural to suppose that when He drew a picture of the harvest in a parable, He intended a similar reference.[4] In terms of this parable, therefore, we must conceive Jesus not as sowing the seed, nor yet as watching the growth and pre-dicting a harvest in the future, but as standing in the presence of the ripe crop, and taking active steps to "put in the sickle." *That* is what the Kingdom of God is like. It is the fulfilment of the process. If we then ask, Who sowed the seed? we may answer, The sowing is that initial act of God which is prior to all human activity, the "prevenient grace" which is the con-dition of anything good happening among men.[5] The stages of growth however are visible. We know that Jesus regarded His work as the fulfilment of the work of the prophets, and that He saw in the success of John the Baptist a sign that the power of God was at work.[6] Thus the parable would suggest that the crisis which has now arrived is the climax of a long process which prepared the way for it.

This interest in the providential antecedents of His work is thoroughly characteristic of the teaching of Jesus. The parable lays stress upon the fact that growth is a mysterious process independent of the will or act of man. We may recall

[4] Similarly Cadoux, *op. cit.*, pp. 162-164.
[5] I owe this to a suggestion of the late Sir Edwyn Hoskyns.
[6] See also pp. 31-33.

that Jesus put to His adversaries the question, "The Baptism of John, was it of heaven or of men?" (Mk. xi. 30), the implied answer being that it was an act of God. The traditional symbol of harvest is thus given a fresh turn. The parable in effect says, Can you not see that the long history of God's dealings with His people has reached its climax? After the work of the Baptist only one thing remains: "Put ye in the sickle, for the harvest is ripe."

Let us now consider whether the other parables of growth are susceptible of interpretation along similar lines.

The parable of the Sower (Mk. iv. 2-8)[7] has come down to us with an elaborate interpretation on allegorical lines. It is not necessary, after Jülicher,[8] to show once again that the interpretation is not consistent with itself, and does not really fit the parable. But it is worth while observing that it is a striking example of the way in which the early Church re-interpreted sayings and parables of Jesus to suit its changing needs. The interpretation assumes a long period during which the effectiveness and genuineness of Christian belief are tested by "the cares of the world and the deceitfulness of riches," and by "persecution and affliction because of the Word." The parable is made to yield warning and encouragement to Christians under such conditions. The interpretation is indeed a moving sermon upon the parable as text. It generalizes the application thoroughly. The sower sows the word. It is not suggested that Christ Himself is the Sower. Any faithful Christian preacher is a sower. He will find much of his work wasted. Some hearers will never grasp the truth effectively at all. Others will be discouraged by difficulties, beguiled by prosperity. Yet the preacher may be sure that in the end there will be results from his labours. This homiletic style is unlike what we know of the teaching of Jesus. In trying to understand the parable we shall do well to leave it aside.

[7] Otto (Reich Gottes und Menschensohn, pp. 90 sqq.) suggested that the parable of the Sower originally formed a unity with that of the Seed growing Secretly. This is an arbitrary reconstruction, and it is contrary to what we know of the history of the tradition to suppose that a single parable was separated into simpler units. The tendency was in the opposite direction.

[8] Gleichnisreden Jesu, II, 1910, pp. 514-538.

In later exegesis it has usually been assumed that by the Sower we must understand Jesus Himself. A favourite line of interpretation is to suggest that He is in effect thinking aloud about the fortunes of His work in Galilee, with its mixture of failure and success. There is much to be said for this. It does give point and actuality to the parable if we no longer generalize it, but insistent upon relating it to the existing situation during the life of Jesus. But I think that something even more pointed and precise is called for. The " eschatological " school, rightly, as I think, lays the stress where it falls in the parable as told, upon the abundant crop; but when they proceed to apply it to the sudden breaking-in of the Kingdom of God which they suppose Jesus to have expected in the near future, they do not seem to me to be keeping closely to the *data.*

Let us take the parable as it stands, forgetting the interpretation entirely—as few modern exegetes do forget it, even though they may accept Jülicher's demonstration of its secondary character. We have the story of a farmer's fortunes. He sows broadcast. Inevitably much of the seed is lost for various reasons; the birds, the thorns, and the rocky ground are objects familiar to every farmer, illustrating the kind of thing with which he has to reckon. They are part of the dramatic machinery of the story, not to be interpreted symbolically. But no farmer despairs because of such inevitable waste of labour and seed: it is to be expected; in spite of all, he may have an excellent harvest.

Now Jesus, I have suggested, in the parable of the Seed growing Secretly, pointed his hearers to the facts of past and present history as showing that the time has come when the gains of the whole process may be realized. The crop is ripe; it is time to reap. But, they might have objected, even the work of John the Baptist has not brought about that complete " restoration of all things " (Mk. ix. 12) which was anticipated as the immediate prelude to the Day of the Lord. Much of his work, as of the work of all the prophets, has been a failure. True, says Jesus; but no farmer yet delayed to reap a good crop because there were bare patches in the field. In spite of all, the harvest is plentiful: it is only the labourers that are lacking. " Pray the Lord of the harvest to send labourers into His harvest."

The parable of the Tares is peculiar to Matthew (xiii. 24-30), and is often supposed to be that evangelist's elaboration of the Marcan parable of the Seed growing Secretly. This does not seem to me in the least probable. The Matthæan parable stands on its own feet. It depicts in characteristic fashion a perfectly perspicuous situation. The interpretation indeed which Matthew has annexed is even more obviously secondary than the Marcan interpretation of the Sower, by which it was probably suggested. In addition to the homiletic or " paræ-netic " motive which is dominant in Mark, it shows the " escha-tological " motive at work. The lesson taught is that there are good and bad members of the Church (the Kingdom of the Son of Man), and that it is not the Lord's will that any attempt should be made to expel the bad before the final judgment. We may compare Paul's protest : " Judge nothing before the time, until the Lord come, who will also bring to light the things that darkness hides, and make manifest the counsels of hearts " (I Cor. iv. 5).

This injunction is supported by a vivid picture of the " con-summation of the age." " The Son of Man will send His angels, and they will collect out of His Kingdom all scandals and all who do iniquity; and they will cast them into the furnace of fire; there shall be weeping and gnashing of teeth. Then the righteous will shine like the sun in the kingdom of their Father." This is the developed eschatology of the Church, as we have it also in the Matthæan parable (so-called) of the Sheep and Goats, and scarcely anywhere else in the Gospels. We shall do well to forget this interpretation as completely as possible. There is no sign that it has had any effect upon the actual form of the story, which runs as follows.

" The kingdom of heaven is like a man who sowed good seed in his field. But while men were asleep, his enemy came and sowed tares among the wheat. When the blades sprouted and produced fruit, then the tares appeared too. The householder's slaves came and said to him, ' Sir, did you

not sow good seed in your field? How is it that it contains
tares?' He replied ' An enemy has done this.' The slaves
said, ' Do you wish us to go and gather them?' He said ' No :
in gathering the tares you might uproot the wheat as well.
Let both grow together till harvest and at harvest time I
will say to the reaper; Gather the tares first, and tie them in
bundles to burn them; but pile the wheat in my barn.' "

It is a realistic story of agricultural life, told vividly and
naturally. Attention is fixed upon the moment at which the
farmer becomes aware that there are weeds among his corn.
The spiteful act of his enemy is a part of the dramatic
machinery of the story and has no independent significance.
He regrets the weeds, but is quite content to leave things as
they are, knowing that the harvest will provide opportunity
for separating wheat and weeds.

Now we have seen that in the parable of the Seed Growing
Secretly Jesus may be supposed to have referred to the work
of God as manifested in the growth of true religion before
His ministry, and particularly to the ministry of John the
Baptist; and that in the parable of the Sower He is implicitly
answering an objection : the Kingdom of God cannot be here
yet, because all Israel has not repented. The parable of the
Tares might fitly be a reply to a similar objection. There
are many sinners in Israel : how can it be that the Kingdom
of God has come? The answer is : As little as a farmer delays
his reaping when harvest-time is come, because there are
weeds among the crop, so little does the coming of the Kingdom
of God delay because there are sinners in Israel. The coming of
the Kingdom is itself a process of sifting, a judgment.

If this is right, then the point of view is slightly different
from that which I have assumed for the other two parables;
for here the harvest has not yet actually begun. I do not
however think that there is any real inconsistency. As we have
seen, the coming of the Kingdom of God is in the teaching of
Jesus not a momentary event, but a complex of interrelated
events including His own ministry, His death, and what follows,
all conceived as forming a unity. Within this complex unity
there is room for different points of view. It is characteristic
of the parable as such that it can dramatize only one point

of view. In order that the intermixture of good and evil in
Israel may be vividly illustrated, it is necessary to have a picture
of the field with wheat and tares growing side by side, before the
harvest begins. It does not seem necessary to suppose that the
judgment is treated as a new event in the future.

It seems possible therefore to give to these parables a consistent and pointed application to the historical situation;
one which does justice to the emphasis laid upon the processes
of growth, and yet does not contemplate a long period of development after the death of Jesus. All three illustrate in
various ways the coming of the Kingdom of God in the ministry
of Jesus, under the figure of harvest.

Significantly enough, this interpretation finds support in the
Fourth Gospel. The Johannine equivalent for the Synoptic
saying, " The harvest truly is plenteous " is to be found in
the words, " Lift up your eyes and behold the fields, that they
are white unto harvest " (Jn. iv. 35). The whole context reads
as follows :

" Do you not say, ' Four months yet, and the harvest
comes.'[9] Behold I say to you, lift up your eyes and observe
the fields, that they are white for harvest. Already the
reaper is taking his pay, and gathering a crop for eternal
life, so that sower and reaper may rejoice together. For in
this the saying is true : ' One sows and another reaps.' I
sent you to reap that on which you have not laboured.
Others have laboured, and you have entered into their
labour " (iv. 35-38).

The purport of this is clear. Jesus sends His disciples (as
in Mt. ix. 38-39; Lk. x. 1-2) not to sow but to reap. The labour
which prepared for the harvest has all been done, and done
by others (we must think of " the prophets until John "). Now
harvest-time has come. Here, as in other cases, John is a true

[9] This I take to be a quasi-proverbial maxim : four months from
seed-time to harvest. The disciples are conceived as thinking that the
" harvest " (i.e. the coming of the Kingdom of God) is still in the
future. Jesus says, " No; if you used your eyes you could see the tokens
of its coming all around you—put in the sickle, for the harvest is
ripe !"

interpreter of the tradition lying behind the Synoptics, the more so because for him the reconstructed eschatology of the early Church has no more interest.

It will be well here to consider a parable which Matthew gives as companion to that of the Tares, and with a similar interpretation—the parable of the Dragnet. The parable runs as follows:

> "The kingdom of heaven is like a drag-net which was cast into the sea and gathered (fish) of every kind; and when it was full, they drew it up to shore, and sat down and collected the good (fish) into receptacles, but threw the bad away" (xiii. 47-48).

Matthew has found here an allegory of the Last Judgment. This is clearly secondary and may be ignored. What, then, is the real point of the parable? We have already found a clue to the parables of harvest in the saying with which Jesus prepared His followers for their mission. I suggest that we may similarly find a clue to this parable in the words He spoke to the fishermen whom he called to follow Him: "Follow me, and I will make you fishers of men" (Mk. i. 17). From this we know that Jesus used fishing as a metaphor for the work which He and His disciples were doing. It is natural to suppose that a parable about fishing carries out the same metaphor. Now the point of the story is that when you are fishing with a drag-net you cannot expect to select your fish: your catch will be a mixed one: "all is fish that comes to your net," as our proverb has it. Similarly, the fishers of men must be prepared to cast their net widely over the whole field of human society. We are then reminded of the parable of the Great Feast, in which the invitation is given to all chance passers-by in highways and lanes. The mission of Jesus and His disciples involves an undiscriminating appeal to men of every class and type.

But—there is after all a process of selection[10]; and this we may aptly illustrate from a series of Gospel *pericopæ* in which

[10] Similarly Cadoux, *op. cit.*, pp. 27 sqq.

there is a sifting of possible followers of Jesus. A rich man comes, doing obeisance to Jesus and asking the way to life: he is tested by the call to abandon his riches, and fails (Mk. x. 17-22). Another offers to follow Jesus anywhere, and is warned—" the Son of Man has nowhere to lay His head ". Another is called to follow, but pleads for time to bury his father: " Let the dead bury their dead," is the stern reply. Yet another wishes to go home to say good-bye, and is warned: " No man who puts his hand to the plough and looks back is fit for the Kingdom of God " (Lk. ix. 57-62). This is the process of selection indicated in the parable of the Drag-net. The appeal goes to all and sundry: the worthy are separated from the unworthy by their reaction to the demands which the appeal involves.

Here then we have an interpretation of the parable which brings it into line with other sayings of Jesus, and relates it to the actual course of His ministry. The Kingdom of God, in process of realization in and through that ministry, is like the work of fishing with a drag-net, for the appeal is made to all indiscriminately, and yet in the nature of things it is selective; and, let us recall, this selection *is* the divine judgment, though men pass it upon themselves by sheer ultimate attitude to the appeal.

We now turn to another parable of growth—the parable of the Mustard Seed, which is found both in Mark and in the material common to Matthew and Luke. The main features of the parable are identical in both forms. The Marcan version runs as follows:

" How shall we liken the Kingdom of God, or in what comparison shall we place it? It is like a mustard-seed, which when it was sown on the ground—being, as it is, smaller than all seeds on the ground—when it is sown, it shoots up and becomes greater than all herbs and puts out great branches, so that the birds of the air can roost under its shadow " (iv. 30-32).

The " Q " version can best be recovered from Luke, since

Matthew (xiii. 31-32), in accordance with his general custom, has conflated his two sources:

> "What is the Kingdom of God like, and to what shall I liken it? It is like a mustard-seed which a man sowed in his garden, and it grew and became a tree and the birds of the air roosted in its branches" (Lk. xiii. 18-19).

The emphasis on the smallness of the seed is in Mark alone,[11] and is probably intrusive. If we neglect it, then the main point of the parable is not the contrast between small beginnings and great results. In both forms the prevailing idea is that of growth up to a point at which the tree can shelter the birds. There is a clear reference to O.T. passages (Dan. iv. 12; Ezek. xxxi. 6, xvii. 23[12]), where a tree sheltering the birds is a symbol for a great empire offering political protection to its subject-states. Since this element belongs to the earliest tradition to which we can hope to have access—that which lies behind the divergent traditions of Mark and "Q"—we shall do well to assume that it is a clue to the application originally intended.

If now we follow the general principle laid down for the interpretation of the parables of Growth—that the Kingdom of God is compared to the harvest—we must suppose that in this parable Jesus is asserting that the time has come when the blessings of the Reign of God are available for all men The parable then falls into line with that of the Great Feast

---

[11] The clause μικρότερον ὂν πάντων τῶν σπερμάτων τῶν ἐπὶ τῆς γῆς has disturbed the grammar of the sentence. Moreover, the mustard-seed is not the smallest seed in common use. The evangelist seems to have interpolated a clause to indicate the sense in which he understood the parable; the Church is a small affair in its beginnings, but it is the germ of the universal Kingdom of God.

[12] Ezek. xvii. 22-23. "I will also take of the lofty top of the cedar, and will set it; I will crop off from the topmost of his young twigs a tender one, and I will plant it upon an high mountain and eminent; in the mountain of the height of Israel will I plant it; and it shall bring forth boughs, and bear fruit, and be a goodly cedar; and under it shall dwell all fowl of every wing; in the shadow of the branches thereof shall they dwell"; a strongly eschatological passage referring to the future glory of Israel, which otherwise described (as in *Assumption of Moses*, x. 1 sqq.) as the appearance of the Kingdom of God.

to which tag-rag-and-bobtail were invited, and with all those
sayings which justify the appeal of Jesus to publicans and
sinners.[13] That multitudes of the outcast and neglected in
Israel, perhaps even of Gentiles, are hearing the call, is a sign
that the process of obscure development is at an end. The
Kingdom of God is here: the birds are flocking to find
shelter in the shade of the tree.

In "Q" (Mt. xiii. 33=Lk. xiii. 20-21) the parable of the
Mustard-seed has for companion that of the Leaven, instead
of that of the Seed Growing Secretly, as in Mark. If the
parable of the Leaven stood originally in this connection, then
we should have to seek for an interpretation on the lines already
suggested for the parable of the Mustard-seed. In that case
the emphasis must lie upon the completion of the process of
fermentation. The period of obscure development is over; the
dough is completely leavened: the Kingdom of God, for
which the prophets until John made preparation, has now
come.

We cannot, however, be sure that the parable of the Leaven
was originally attached to that of the Mustard Seed. As we
have seen, pairs of parables are characteristic of the tradition
of the teaching of Jesus, but the pairs are not always constant.[14]
This is a case in point. The original pair may have been,
Seed Growing Secretly with Mustard Seed, as in Mark, leaving
the Leaven as a parable by itself.

Now if that parable stood alone, and we were seeking to
interpret it without help from a companion parable, the
above is not the view of its meaning which would naturally
suggest itself. "Leaven" is, in general, a symbol for evil
influences carrying infection.[15] In this sense Jesus used it
when He spoke of the leaven of the Pharisees (Mk. viii. 15
and parallels). By analogy, it should be used here as a symbol
for a wholesome influence, propagating itself similarly by a
kind of infection. In that case we should be obliged to suppose
that when the Kingdom of God is compared to leaven, the

[13] See pp. 90-95.
[14] See pp. 85, 87, 90-92, 135.
[15] As in I Cor. v. 6; Gal. v. 9; similarly in Rabbinic literature for
the "evil inclination." See Strack-Billerbeck on Mt. xvi. 6.

suggestion is that the ministry of Jesus is itself such an influence. This, which approximates to the current interpretation of the parable, may have been its original intention, if it had no essential connection with the parable of the Mustard Seed. We should observe that the working of the leaven in dough is not a slow, imperceptible process. At first, it is true, the leaven is " hidden," and nothing appears to happen; but soon the whole mass swells and bubbles, as fermentation rapidly advances. The picture, I think, is true to history. The ministry of Jesus was like that. There was in it no element of external coercion, but in it the power of God's Kingdom worked from within, mightily permeating the dead lump of religious Judaism in His time. The nearest parallel to this parable among the non-parabolic sayings seems to be the Lucan passage, xvii. 20-21 : " The Kingdom of God does not come by looking for it, nor shall they say, ' Look here! Look there '; for the Kingdom of God is within you."[16]

The parables of growth, then, are susceptible of a natural interpretation which makes them into a commentary on the actual situation during the ministry of Jesus, in its character as the coming of the Kingdom of God in history. They are not to be taken as implying a long process of development introduced by the ministry of Jesus and to be consummated by his second advent, though the Church later understood them in that sense. As in the teaching of Jesus as a whole, so here, there is no long historical perspective : the *eschaton*, the divinely ordained climax of history, is here. It has come by no human effort, but by act of God; and yet not by an arbitrary, catastrophic intervention, for it is the harvest following upon a long process of growth. This is the element which these parables introduced. The coming of the Kingdom is indeed a crisis brought by divine intervention : but it is not an unprepared crisis, unrelated to the previous course of history. An obscure process of growth has gone before it, and the fresh act of God which calls the crisis into being is an answer to the work of God in history which has gone before. In Jewish apocalypse, although the metaphor of harvest is used, there is

[16] If this is the meaning of Lk. xvii, 21. See p. 62, n. 4.

little or no sense of any organic relation between the processes of history and its culmination. The divine event is an unrelated and unconditioned intervention. It is not so in the teaching of Jesus. Having come, however, the Kingdom does call for human effort. The harvest waits for reapers, and it is in this light that Jesus sets His own work and that to which He calls His disciples.

Chapter VII

CONCLUSIONS

It may perhaps have seemed that by ruling out any interpretation of the parables which gives them a general application, and insisting upon their intense particularity as comments upon an historical situation, we have reduced their value as instruments of religious teaching, and left them with no more than an historical interest. The parables, however, have an imaginative and poetical quality. They are works of art, and any serious work of art has significance beyond its original occasion. No pedantry of exegesis could ever prevent those who have " ears to hear," as Jesus said, from finding that the parables "speak to their conditions."[1] Their teaching may be fruitfully applied and re-applied to all sorts of new situations which were never contemplated at the time when they were spoken. But a just understanding of their original import in relation to a particular situation in the past will put us on right lines in applying them to our own new situations.

This point may be illustrated in relation to the parables of growth. The metaphor of seed time and harvest is a very natural and a very common image for various aspects of the religious life. In particular, from Paul onward, with his " I planted, Apollos watered, but God gives the increase,"[2] this metaphor has frequently been applied to the work of the Church and its ministers in the world. It may be used to remind the servant of God that his task is the humble and yet important task of " sowing the word "—that is, of declaring the truth committed to him and leaving it to work. It may be used to inculcate patience, since growth is a very gradual process and cannot be hurried—" First the blade, then the ear, then the full corn in the ear." It may be used to give encouragement

[1] I may refer to what I have said about the universal and the particular in O.T. prophecy in *The Authority of the Bible*, pp. 124-128.
[2] I Cor. iii. 6.

under seeming failure; in spite of predictory birds, thorns, and stony places, there will yet be a crop.

All these and, no doubt, many others are legitimate applications of the metaphor. But if it be true that Jesus Himself originally used it in the sense that His followers were called to reap a harvest which by grace of God was ready for the sickle, then the Christian minister may apply it to his own work in a very definite sense. It assures him that he is not called upon to bring the truth of God to an alien world, which apart from his effort presents only bare and barren furrows. The grace of God has been before him. The world into which he is sent is alive with divine energies: "spontaneously the earth bears fruit." It is his task to claim for God that which His grace has prepared. A real understanding and acceptance of this truth is of importance for the whole attitude of the Church to the world, and for the spirit in which its ministers undertake their work.

In this way, if we wish to generalize the teaching of the parables, we shall do well to be guided by their original and particular application. But after all, that particular application is itself of the first importance, if we believe that the Christian religion rests upon the "finished work" of Christ, that is, to speak in terms of historical fact, upon the events narrated and interpreted in the Gospels. For, if the argument of this book is right, the parables represent the interpretation which our Lord offered of His own ministry.

It appears that while Jesus employed the traditional symbolism of apocalypse to indicate the "other-worldly" or absolute character of the Kingdom of God, He used parables to enforce and illustrate the idea that the Kingdom of God had come upon men there and then. The inconceivable had happened: history had become the vehicle of the eternal; the absolute was clothed with flesh and blood. Admittedly, it was a "mystery," to be understood by those who have eyes to see and ears to hear, by those to whom it is revealed "not by flesh and blood, but by My Father in heaven."

It is in this context that the parables of the Kingdom of God must be placed. They use all the resources of dramatic illustration to help men to see that in the events before their eyes —in the miracles of Jesus, His appeal to men and its results, the blessedness that comes to those who follow Him, and the hardening of those who reject Him; in the tragic conflict of the Cross, and the tribulation of the disciples; in the fateful choice before the Jewish people, and the disasters that threaten—God is confronting them in His kingdom, power and glory. This world has become the scene of a divine drama, in which the eternal issues are laid bare. It is the hour of decision. It is realized eschatology.

This is the implication of all the parables we have considered. We may now pass them in review, and observe the various aspects of the situation which they emphasize and illustrate.

First, this is the hour of fulfilment. For many generations the faith of the Jewish people had buoyed itself upon the hope that at long last God would assert His sovereignty in His world, while it sadly confessed that in the present age the powers of evil were strong. In a succession of pictures Jesus declares that the hour has struck and God has acted. The strong man is despoiled; the powers of evil are disarmed. The hidden power of God has manifested itself, as the productive energies of the earth bring the harvest in its time. This is not the work of man, any more than man can cause the seed to grow and the grain to ripen. It is the divine initiative. For man, there is the joy of harvest.

Not indeed that there is any spectacular exhibition of divine power. There is no *coup d'état,* and no summoning of legions of angels. There is only a Galilæan Carpenter preaching in the streets and healing the sick. The careless scoff: "Only one more of these religious enthusiasts. We know them: there was John, but he was mad; and now there is Jesus, and he is not even respectable"—like peevish children, said Jesus; but all the same, "the Kingdom of God has come upon you." For there is a power which works from within, like leaven in dough, and nothing can stop it.

Jesus has not come as a religious reformer, to patch up the ragged robe of Pharisaic Judaism (foolish idea! patching would only hasten the end of the old coat). This is a new departure in the relations of God and man; and new especially in that His grace is exhibited to the undeserving. "The Lord loveth the righteous, and His ear is open to their cry," said the old religion. But this is not now the whole story. To whom should the doctor come, if not to the sick? And so the Son of Man, in whom the Kingdom of God comes, is content to be known as " the friend of publicans and sinners." The strayed sheep is the especial object of the shepherd's care, and a frugal housewife will count no trouble too great to recover one lost coin out of her store. So Jesus went about the towns and villages of Galilee, seeking the lost; and that was how the Kingdom of God came. He launched out into the deep, and all was fish that came to His net. Nor was His appeal without results. The outcasts could be seen flocking into the Kingdom of God, as the birds fly to roost in the branches of a stalwart tree (which not long ago was an almost invisible seed). And for those who accepted the Kingdom of God there was pure happiness, like the joy of a wedding-feast.

The appeal and its success caused scandal. Could this be the coming of the Kingdom of God, when all the moral safeguards laboriously built up by the teachers of the Law were cast aside, and the lawless were welcomed into fellowship? To those who raised such objections Jesus appealed in parables with an ironical point. If invited guests do not come to a feast, something must be done to fill the vacant seats. And if a son who made fair promises fails to fulfil them, credit is surely due to the other son who atones for his first rudeness by a tardy obedience. Even if the younger son of a family has dragged his father's name in the mud, it is not for his elder brother to cut him off, if the father is glad to receive him when at last he comes home. But, in fact, there is no such thing as merit in the sight of God. If He bestows His gifts upon men who have done nothing to deserve them, He is like a magnificently generous employer who pays a full day's wage for an hour's work. The Kingdom of God is like that.

Yet the Kingdom of God does come with judgment. The religious leaders, who censured Jesus for His work and teaching, were at that very moment pronouncing judgment upon themselves, by the attitude they displayed, by their self-centred caution, their exclusiveness, their neglect of responsibilities, and their blindness to the purpose of God. In their hands the salt of the religion of Israel had lost its savour, its light was under a bushel. They were like an unprofitable servant who hid his master's money rather than risk it in investment, like an unfaithful steward who abused his trust, like defaulting tenants. This was the moral situation which found dramatic expression in the tragic forebodings of the ruin of the Jewish community and the destruction of the Temple.

In His individual appeals Jesus struck the same sterner note. The very fact that the supreme gift God is offered to men lends an especial significance to the response that they make. The act of acceptance or of rejection determines the whole direction of a man's life, and so of his destiny. The course of events in which the Kingdom of God comes upon men

> " Tends to one moment's product, thus,
>   When a soul declares itself, to wit,
>   By its fruit, the thing it does."

Now that the offer is made, it is impossible to shirk the decision, just as a debtor who is being hauled off to court, or an employee under notice of dismissal, must make up his mind there and then to do something about it, before all opportunity for action is at an end.

As the course of events developed, it became more and more clear that those who responded to the call of Jesus must " count the cost," and the situation itself defined the momentous character of the decision. He had to say to would-be followers, The treasure is within your reach; but what will you pay for it? Not that the blessings of the Kingdom of God can be bought, at any price: they are the gift of God. But because the situation called for sacrifice, it raised the question at issue to the point at which nothing short of absolute sincerity would count. " Will you accept the Kingdom of God?" meant, in view of the facts, " Will you stake your life upon it?"

Thus the coming of the Kingdom of God displayed its character as judgment, that is to say, as the testing and sifting of men. Though a drag-net may bring all kinds of fish to shore, they must be picked over before they can be marketed (as the fishermen-disciples knew well). Harvest is both the ingathering of the crop *and* the separation of wheat and tares. So the multitudes who were brought by the preaching of Jesus within the scope of the Kingdom of God were sifted by the way in which things went. They passed judgment upon themselves, not by introspective self-examination, but by their re-action to the developing situation. For it presently became clear that the opposition to Jesus was irreconcilable. A clash must come. When and how it would come, who could say? Does a householder know when his premises are to be broken into? It is the unexpected that happens. So Jesus was concerned to prepare His hearers for the unexpected. They must be like servants sitting up all night for their master, without knowing when he will come; like bridesmaids whose lamps must be alight whenever the procession starts.

At this point the curtain falls upon the scene illuminated by the parables. For the clash came, with tragic suddenness, and in what followed Jesus no longer taught, but acted and suffered. He died, to rise again. The disciples, taken after all by surprise, forsook Him and fled; but afterwards, they rose out of failure into a new life, and understood how the mystery of the Kingdom of God had been finally revealed in His death and resurrection.

The conviction remains central to the Christian faith, that at a particular point in time and space, the eternal entered decisively into history. An historic crisis occurred by which the whole world of man's spiritual experience is controlled. To that moment in history our faith always looks back. The Gospel is not a statement of general truths of religion, but an interpretation of that which once happened. The Creeds are anchored in history by the clause " under Pontius Pilate." Above all, in the Sacrament of the Eucharist the Church recapitulates the historic crisis in which Christ came, lived, died and rose again, and finds in it the " efficacious sign " of eternal life in the Kingdom of God. In its origin and in its governing ideas it may be described as a sacrament of realized eschatology.[8] The Church prays, " Thy Kingdom come ";

[8] On the eschatological background of the Eucharist, see my article, " The Lord's Supper in the New Testament," in the book *Christian Worship: Studies in its History and Meaning,* edited by N. Micklem (Oxford University Press). The eschatological character of the Sacrament is most clear in the Eastern Rite. In the Liturgy of St. John Chrysostom significant references to the Kingdom of God occur at most points of the service, and apocalyptic and eschatological language is freely used. The " Cherubic Hymn " prays " that we may receive the King of all, invisibly escorted by the Angelic Hosts," thus

"Come, Lord Jesus." As it prays, it remembers that the Lord did come, and with Him came the Kingdom of God. Uniting memory with aspiration, it discovers that He comes. He comes in His Cross and Passion; He comes in the glory of His Father with the holy angels. Each Communion is not a stage in a process by which His coming draws gradually nearer, or a milestone on the road by which we slowly approach the distant goal of the Kingdom of God on earth. It is a re-living of the decisive moment at which He came.

The preaching of the Church is directed towards reconstituting in the experience of individuals the hour of decision which Jesus brought. Its underlying theme is always: "The time is fulfilled and the Kingdom of God has come. Repent, and believe the Gospel." It assumes that history in the individual life is of the same stuff as history at large; that is, it is significant in so far as it serves to bring men face to face with God in His Kingdom, power and glory. We are blind and

---

preparing for the *Sursum Corda* and *Sanctus* (common in substance to all liturgies), which culminate in the announcement (in effect) of the coming of the Son of Man " in the glory of His Father with the holy angels "—" Blessed is He that cometh in the Name of the Lord, Hosanna in the Highest." This leads to the recital of the words of institution and the commemoration of " all that was endured for our sake, the Cross, the Grave, the Resurrection after three days, the Ascension into Heaven, the Enthronement at the right hand of the Father, and the second and glorious Coming again." Then as the Priest proceeds to Communion, he prays, " Hearken, O Lord Jesus Christ our God, from Thy Holy dwelling-place and from the Throne of glory of Thy Kingdom, and come and sanctify us, Thou Who sittest above with the Father and art here invisibly present with us," and again, " Receive me, O Son of God, as a partaker of Thy Mystic Feast . . . Lord, remember me when Thou comest in Thy Kingdom." All through the remembrance of the coming of Christ in history, and the hope of His eternal Kingdom, are inextricably bound together with the sense of His presence with His Church. The worshippers are placed within that moment at which the Kingdom of God came, and experience sacramentally its coming, both as a fact secure within the historical order and as the eternal reality whose full meaning can never be known to men on earth. This eschatological aspect of the Sacrament is partly obscured in the Western liturgies (Roman and Anglican), but it can still be discerned. (Quotations from the Liturgy of St. John Chrysostom are given according to the English translation authorized by the Most Rev. the Metropolitan Germanos, published by the Faith Press, as used in the Cathedral of Holy Wisdom in London.)

deaf, and half a lifetime of our history may pass us by without our discerning any eternal significance in it. Then the moment may come when the eyes of the blind are opened, and the ears of the deaf unstopped. The invitations to the feast are out: "Come, for all is ready!" The bridegroom is home from the wedding, the master from his journey: we must give account of our talents; we must render the produce of our vineyard. Blessed is that servant who is found awake; he enters into the joy of his Lord. The Kingdom of God has come, and he who receives it as a little child shall enter in.

In the same way, in that larger history which is the experience of human society, there may be long periods in which the divine significance of events is hidden from our eyes. We sleep and wake, night and day, while the seed grows, we know not how. Then comes the harvest. From time to time history reveals its momentous meaning, in a crisis which brings a challenge to men. The judgments of the Lord are in the earth. It is the business of the Church, to which is committed the Gospel of the Kingdom of God, to interpret the crisis by the light of that supreme crisis of the past, which is continually made present in Christian experience and worship. In that crisis there was judgment, and conflict, and a cross. The Gospel of the Kingdom of God is not an assurance of peace and happiness on easy terms. It may be God's "No!" pronounced upon things that we have valued. But in the end it runs, "Blessed are ye poor, for yours is the Kingdom of God."

Out of this a Christian view of history emerges. Some students of history see it as a mere succession of occurrences, connected no doubt by a chain of cause and effect, but offering no evidence of design. Others have tried to exhibit it as the field of an orderly evolutionary process, showing advance from lower to higher levels of living, and offering promise of an ultimate perfection of human society on earth.

It is possible for religion to come to terms with either view. For the pure mystic history is a matter of indifference. It may be sheer illusion. But religious thinkers in the West, and especially in this country and in America, have recently tended to attach themselves to the latter school of thought. In the supposed law of progress in history they have seen evidence of the immanent Spirit of God, leading humanity onwards to its goal, which they have identified with the Kingdom of God on earth. This however does not appear to be the view to which the teaching of the Gospels points. There is no hint that the Kingdom of God is Utopia. The restored kingdom of David, which was the Utopia of popular Jewish hopes in the time of Jesus, is all but expressly rejected, and no alternative Utopia is suggested.

The modern Western mind tends to value the historical process for the sake of the goal (still within history) to which by a succession of cause and effect it may ultimately lead. Unless we have interpreted the Gospels quite wrongly, the thought of Jesus passed directly from the immediate situation to the eternal order lying beyond all history, of which He spoke in the language of apocalyptic symbolism. He did not strip history of its value, for He declared that the eternal order was present in the actual situation, and that this situation was the "harvest" of history that had gone before. His teaching therefore is not rightly described as mystical, if we understand the mystic to be one who seeks escape from the moving world of things and events. There remains in His teaching a certain tension between "other-worldliness" and "this-worldliness," represented by the apparent contradiction between the prayer, "Thy Kingdom come," and the declaration, "The Kingdom of God has come upon you." From this tension Christian thought cannot escape, while it is true to its original inspiration.[4]

We seem led to the view that, whether or not history holds within it an immanent necessity to move towards a goal, its primary religious significance is not to be found there. The particularity which is of the essence of actual events is not to be smoothed away by the assumption of any general law governing their occurrence. The "pattern" of history, so far as its spiritual values are concerned, is exhibited in crisis rather than in evolution. Every crisis is a thing by itself, unique and non-recurrent. Consequently, we need not try to reduce all events, great and small, to the same scale, as

[4] Cf. A. Schweitzer, *Christianity and the Religions of the World,* 1923.

elements in a uniform process, governed by general laws, and deriving its significance from the remote goal to which it tends. Events in their particularity have value, and have value in different degrees. Thus we are at liberty to recognize in one particular series of events a crisis of supreme significance, and to interpret other events and situations with reference to it. Christian thought finds this supreme crisis in the ministry and death of Jesus Christ with the immediate sequel. Its supreme significance lies in the fact that here history became the field within which God confronted men in a decisive way, and placed before them a moral challenge that could not be evaded.

This then, from the Christian point of view, is the clue to the significance of history. The series of events is neither a veil of illusion hiding the eternal from our eyes, nor a process working out its own values from within apart from any reference to a timeless reality beyond it. It is instrumental, or more properly sacramental, to the eternal order. The several events in the series, in which the minds, wills and affections of individual men and women are implicated, are each of them capable of confronting these individuals with the Kingdom of God, that is, with the ultimate good and the final power in the universe. Out of their response, one way or the other, further events proceed. Thus history is moulded by the spirit.[5] The whole series of events remains plastic to the will of God, and serves to bring men again and again face to face with the eternal issues.

We cannot predict the results of human choice upon its course beyond, at most, the next stage, because the field of " natural law " in history, though real, is limited, and there is no known calculus of the interaction of timeless spirit with the temporal order.[6] The composition of imaginary " histories " of the next few centuries or millennia, which is so popular at present, is an agreeable form of fiction, and may serve to set in clear relief an analysis of existing tendencies; but it has no relation to the objective course of events. The true prophet always fore-shortens.

[5] On the rhythm observable between the outward course of events and the exercise of spiritual spontaneity, the former providing the conditions of the latter, and the latter in turn shaping the former, see *The Authority of the Bible*, pp. 261-264.
[6] Cf. A. Toynbee, *A Study of History*, I, 1935, pp. 271 sqq.

We have, it appears, no warrant in the teaching of Jesus for affirming that the long cycles of history will lead inevitably to a millennial "Kingdom Come" on earth. But we have warrant for affirming that God comes to meet us in history, and sets before us the open but narrow door into his Kingdom. To accept His Kingdom and to enter in brings blessedness, because the best conceivable thing is that we should be in obedience to the will of God. Such blessedness may be enjoyed here and now, but it is never exhausted in any experience that falls within the bounds of time and space. Our destiny lies in the eternal order, and eye hath not seen, nor ear heard, neither hath it entered into the heart of man, what things the Lord hath prepared for them that love Him.

INDEX

PARABLES DISCUSSED IN DETAIL

PARABLES REFERRED TO

AUTHORS